"John Foreman has chall
It's loaded with a wealth of thought p...
elevate your 'game' to a much higher level."

PAT WILLIAMS
Senior Vice President, *Orlando Magic*,
and Co-Author of *Takeaway*

CONSULTANT, CONSULT!

"*Consultant, Consult!* is filled with common sense ideas. Each idea can be acted on immediately to improve your personal and business presence."

LINDA J. MILLER
Global Liaison for Coaching,
The Ken Blanchard Companies

CONSULTANT, CONSULT!

JOHN E. FOREMAN

Consultant, Consult!

Copyright © 2014 John E. Foreman.

Published in association with Development Planning & Financing Group, Inc.

For more information on DPFG's many consulting services and regional offices, please visit www.dpfg.com or call 949-388-9269.

All rights reserved.

Published in the United States of America.

CONTENTS

Acknowledgments, X

As We Begin . . . , XI

Part 1 — Working with Clients, 2

1. Listening Skills Are a Must, 3
2. Always Support Your Client, 5
3. Pick Up the Phone and Talk to the Client the Old-Fashioned Way, 7
4. Know How to Scope a Job, 9
5. Always Prepare for Client Meetings, 11
6. Be Confident with a Client and Rely on Firm Resources, 13
7. Referrals from Existing Clients Are the Key to Success, 16
8. Take Client Bills Personally, 18
9. Take Client Budgets Seriously, 20
10. Clients Do Review Their Bills, 22
11. When Is a Job Sold and When Should You Start Working on It?, 24
12. What Should Be in a Client Engagement Letter?, 26
13. Some Other Not So Obvious Ways of Selling Client Services, 29
14. Watch out for Contract Snafus, 31

15. Why Do Clients Hire Consultants?, 33

16. What Does Your Client Think about You?, 35

Part 2 — Working with a Team, 39

17. Watch Out When the Internal and External Views of a Person Are Radically Different, 41

18. Be a Team Player, Not a Lone Star Cowboy or Cowgirl, 43

19. Don't Work in a Vacuum, 45

20. Pass Your Knowledge Down to Others in Your Company, 47

21. How Do Teams Succeed?, 48

22. What Is a Team Leader Expected to Do?, 51

23. Establish a Solid Review Process, 53

Part 3 — Implementing Strategy, 57

24. Create an Intense But Low Stress Work Environment, 59

25. Be a Fortune Teller, 61

26. Always Identify Client Opportunities, 62

27. Always Know Where You're Going—No Joyriding, 65

28. Know Fact from Fiction, 66

29. Think Like an Entrepreneur, Not a Professor, 68

30. Always Surround Your Consulting Services Around These Things, 70

31. Don't Play the Consulting Chaos Game Like Others, 72

32. You've Got to Get Organized, 73

33. What Are You Doing to Grow the Company?, 75

34. Of Course Those Are Good Ideas, But Which Is the Best?, 77

35. Clearly Understand the Risk/Reward Model, 79

36. Everything Is Negotiable to a Point, 81

37. Set Short-, Mid-, and Long-Term Professional Goals, 84

38. Understand the Forrest Before You Look at the Trees, 86

39. What Are the Attributes of Selling Work?, 88

40. Quickly Understand Your Company's Business Philosophy, 89

41. Focus on Your Offense and Minimize Your Defense, 91

42. Cut Your Losses Sooner than Later, 92

43. How Do You Beat the Competition?, 94

44. Avoid the Sheep Herd, 95

Part 4 — Working Smart, 97

45. One Time Right! No Badminton Please!, 99

46. Know What You Know and Know What You Don't, 101

47. Operate in a Continuous Questioning Mode, 103

48. So You Can't Work Without a Computer, 105

49. Say It in 10 Meaningful Words or Less, 107

50. Memory Is a Must, 109

51. Get Done Now, Not Later, 110

52. When Your Attitude or Patience Gets Thin, Get More Sleep or Take a Vacation, 112

53. Where's Your "To Do" List?, 114

54. Monitor Your Stress Level, 116

55. You Can't Be Shy or Insecure in This Business, 118

56. Establish Low, Mid, and High Mental Gears When Working with Clients, 119

57. These Things Will Get You Fired, 122

58. Are You Being Reasonably Productive?, 124

59. Don't Reinvent the Wheel, 126

60. Drill the Job to Its Fullest, 128

61. Don't Give Information—Get It, 130

62. Don't Build a Mountain Out of a Mole Hill, 133

63. Write Your Business Biography Now, 135

64. Teach with Analogies and Parables, 137

Part 5 — Pursuing Excellence, 141

65. How Did You Make a Difference Today?, 143

66. Your Name and Your Reputation Are All You Have, 145

67. Be Short on Excuses and Long on Responsibility, 146

68. Continually Develop New Ideas—Don't Just Rely on Old Ones, 148

69. Always Lead, 150

70. Never Say or Do These Things in Business, 152

71. Always Exceed Client Expectations, 154

72. Don't Take on Work You Cannot Finish on Time, 156

73. The Incremental Difference Will Set You Apart from Others, 158

74. You're Only as Good as Your Last Job— Accept It and Move On, 159

75. Aptitude Is Everything, But Actually Nothing If You Don't Put It into Action, 161

About the Author, 164

About Development Planning & Financing Group, 166

What Others Say, 167

ACKNOWLEDGMENTS

I want to personally thank upper management at the national accounting firm of Kenneth Leventhal & Company. Ken Leventhal (deceased), Stan Ross, and Michael Meyer inspired me and challenged me to believe and put into practice the concept that you can solve any problem in the real estate industry if you are prepared to think long enough and work hard enough on it.

I also want to thank Jack Oldham and Richard Shapiro for sharing their masterful thoughts and creativity toward problem-solving with me.

AS WE BEGIN . . .

The purpose of this book is to provide you, the reader, with a framework of ideas and concepts for self-evaluation. It is designed to allow you to determine if you have the necessary 75 characteristics in place for growing and succeeding as a consultant (or as an employee in just about any other business).

Though many of the chapters in this book focus on and discuss business-to-business interaction as a consultant, the same ideas and concepts, such as "One Time Right! No Badminton Please," "Always Know Where You're Going—No Joyriding," or "Be Short on Excuses and Long on Responsibility" can easily apply to any employee within a company ranging from the janitor to the president.

I've written this book based on the real-world work experiences I have encountered over the past 32 years in the consulting business. In fact, I have personally applied and transferred the ideas and concepts in this book to others within the national real estate consulting firm Development Planning & Financing Group, Inc., that I co-founded with Peter Piller. The information in this book is the same material that has been instrumental in contributing to the significant growth of the company and its employees.

Now, for the first time, I am sharing on a broad scale these concepts that have proven to serve the private consulting firm so well. This book provides a series of attributes—or do's and don'ts—that when applied in your business will undoubtedly increase your personal and economic value in today's workforce.

As wonderful as our education system is in the United States, the curriculum seems to fall short of teaching the content in this book. This book can serve to help bridge the gap between formal education and the working world for young students or it can serve as a refresher course for those that are already in the working world, seeking to polish and improve their personal economic growth and development.

In many ways, this book can be viewed as a tool to help increase your personal and/or company's competitiveness in business. With globalization upon us, the world's workforce is seeking to fill job positions within U.S. companies. More than ever, prudent workers must differentiate themselves with all the necessary attributes to increase their productivity and value. Those that fail to realize this and act upon it will be left behind.

In a global sense, the consulting business is a major part of the burgeoning service sector trend in the United States, as well as the rest of the world. In the U.S., a growing percentage of our workforce is employed in the service sector and this trend will only continue to increase as our national economy weans itself away from manufacturing jobs that will continue to go overseas.

Simply put, today's workforce is more than ever tied to interacting with other people on a day-to-day service-related basis than with the handling of tangible manufacturing products, so competition in this area will only increase over time.

Every sector in the national and global economy has the need for consultants to assist companies in their day-to-day business operations, and as demand for these services grow so will the competition. There are real estate consultants, software consultants, environmental consultants, scientific consultants, political consultants, sales consultants, and more. Individual and corporate consultants must find core attributes that distinguish them from the competition.

An excellent product in a good market can go a long way, but it seems the ultimate foundation of a company's success is its employees, culture, and passion. How will those consultants or employees perform their jobs when faced with a down business cycle? Will they recoil and go home early and blame the bad business cycle for their lack of performance, or will they understand that tougher business cycles require them to draw more deeply into core attributes, such as those in this book, to thrive and succeed? The true test of character is exemplified not when everything is smooth sailing but when things are stormy and uncertain.

There is so much to learn from a consultant who performs his or her job well, and these lessons are certainly transferable to any employee or business. A consultant may be one of the best test cases to put under a microscope when seeking to find excellence in the workplace because they seem to have the fewest guarantees relative to other employment opportunities; this usually eliminates complacency.

Additionally, consultants know more than anyone else that their client wants to see bottom-line results from their work; by definition, this keeps a consultant focused. The consultant's approach to business is closely aligned to the fundamentals of capitalism in that the consultant gets paid to perform a service for the benefit of a company and the company, in turn, pays for this service during and upon completion. If the cost of paying the consultant does not more than outweigh the benefit received by the company as a result of the consultant's work, it is likely that the consultant will not continue to derive work from that company in the future. Obviously, the benefit received by the company may consist of more than just monetary benefits, but the monetary benefits do rank high in terms of importance to the company.

For some strange reason, many consultants don't grasp this basic concept of value-added consulting. Part of the reason is due to formal education not teaching this business concept. Usually a consultant is hired by a company for a multitude of reasons that range from the belief that their own employees cannot properly do the job well, to not having enough employee horsepower to meet the job deadline.

Many consultants fall into the trap of believing that developing interpersonal relationships with key people in the company will ensure a continuous flow of work from the company. They fail to realize that most companies believe that consultants are replaceable and management has an obligation to its stakeholders to ensure they are procuring outside consulting jobs in the most economical manner possible.

Beyond that, a large percentage of consultants fall into the trap of thinking that it is acceptable to blend in like a company employee when performing a consulting engagement. While it's extremely important to gel with company employees and management when performing work, it's also important to distinguish yourself as being different from the company employee.

The consultant that holds his or her professionalism in the highest regard, and always strives to display technical competency in the proper settings, and utilizes many other ideas and concepts in this book, may find that the company doesn't view him or her as replaceable but rather as irreplaceable.

This concept of value-added consulting is not just limited to consultants, as it can also be used by any employee within any company. Value-added consulting is also not one simple idea. Instead, it's a basket of ideas ranging from economics to human psychology.

The content in this book focuses on real-world experiences by describing and discussing the importance of reliability, inquisitiveness, creativeness, intelligence, memory, preparation, leadership, group participation, organization, confidence, assertiveness, goal setting, energy, and many more key ideas.

This book will challenge you to look within and determine if you have—or want to obtain—the foundational pieces for being a great consultant or employee within any company working within the U.S. It also challenges employers to recognize and reward great consultants or employees within its company.

A practical way to implement the ideas and concepts in this book is to understand that they will not come to fruition overnight. Set realistic goals and reevaluate achievements periodically. Think of the accomplishments you obtain from the ideas and concepts in this book as a series of steps on a stairway—take one step at a time.

Any achievements you obtain from the content of this book will undoubtedly increase your personal value in terms of character and economics, as well as your company's value. So, what are you waiting for? *Consultant, consult!*

PART I
WORKING WITH CLIENTS

CONSULTANT, CONSULT!

PART 1: WORKING WITH CLIENTS

 ## Listening Skills Are a Must

Most people are good listeners when engaged in a discussion in which they are genuinely interested. How many times have you dosed off in a conversation you are *not* interested in having? Probably a lot more times than you would care to admit. If you have a tendency to talk while others are talking, you probably have weak listening skills. You may also be considered rude and inconsiderate. After all, how can you have a meaningful discussion with someone if you don't listen to what they are trying to say to you? You simply cannot!

Great consultants have great listening skills. Client meetings are a great testing ground for determining how well you listen. Before you give your clients advice, it is extremely important to carefully listen to what they have to say. I like to start off client meetings with simple questions that are aimed at getting them to talk about the project and their issues at hand. Most clients will give you a keen sense of the situation at hand and its associated problems. Listening first to the clients ensures that I fully understand their needs, issues and objectives.

Experience has taught me that the advice I will give to the client will be at its fullest potential when I follow this process of listening first and advising second. If an associate consultant within your company is also present in the client meeting, then take time after the meeting to have the associate describe what they heard at the meeting. This will allow you to evaluate the listening skills of the associate, while filling in any details you may have missed.

CONSULTANT, CONSULT!

Being a good listener is extremely important in any consulting venue. I cannot tell you how many negotiation meetings I have been involved in where the person negotiating is not paying careful attention to the opposing side's responses. They are simply doing too much talking and not enough listening. I have seen the negotiating consultant fail to reconcile differences that would be easily reconcilable if the consultant listened carefully to the opposing side's point of view.

One time I came out of a meeting with a client of mine who was convinced that the issue we were negotiating was a dead issue. During the meeting, I noticed that my client was talking too much and not listening to what the opposition was saying. After the meeting, I strongly disagreed with my client that the issue was dead, telling him instead that I thought we were actually at the point of reaching an agreement with the other side. My reasoning was based solely on what was said in the meeting. The client was surprised when I mentioned some of the things discussed in the meeting, because he did not hear what I heard.

Thankfully, the client agreed to meet with the opposing side one more time and at that meeting the parties reached a mutually acceptable agreement on the issue in dispute. I attribute the success of reaching this important agreement to my listening skills. I kept listening to the other side's issues and concerns and developed a strategic solution that would work for my client *and* the opposing side.

Being talkative in client meetings or negotiations is equally as important as being a good listener. So at some point in the course of the meeting you need to move beyond just listening to talking and advising based on what you heard.

PART 1: WORKING WITH CLIENTS

2 Always Support Your Client

In business it's extremely important to interact with customers in a supporting manner. You should always give customers the benefit of the doubt and listen carefully to their needs and ideas. By asking questions, you can help clarify the customer's goals and objectives. You must not lose touch with the reality that you are dealing with just one task or transaction with the customer, out of a multitude of their tasks and transactions. The consultant, by definition, better know more about the task or transaction than the customer. After all that's why they're paying for your consulting services.

I use a containment approach with customers. I allow them to drive the overall direction and approach while I process and provide them the supporting information they need. If the customer's approach strays too much in the wrong direction, I step in and increase my level of participation on direction and approach in the spirit of keeping the process on track.

Most customers generally heed their consultant's advice because they trust the consultant has greater requisite experience on the subject. However, there are times when the results of the process don't come out the way the consultant or the customer wanted. Most customers understand and can accept this as normal business risk that's implicit in most business transactions.

However, from time-to-time you will run into a customer who views you as an expendable tool and in some cases will not hesitate to disrespect you or throw you under the bus. The primary reason this happens is that the employee is concerned he or she may lose their job for not getting the desired result. When the customer crosses the line and openly shows disrespect to you for no valid reason, you must know how to respond.

If the disrespect conveyed could damage your professionalism, you must firmly and openly set the record straight. It takes a long time to earn your professional reputation and credibility, so never let anyone—even a customer—tarnish these qualities. Many consultants will stand by and let their customer take advantage of them because the customer is paying their bill and they have been told customers are always right.

Again, remember your professional reputation is priceless and never let one client compromise your reputation—no matter how big of a bill they are paying. In order to defend yourself in these circumstances, use the power of your critical thinking skills and the facts at hand to put the customer back in a position of respecting you.

In most cases, your customer will respect you for showing backbone relative to the situation, especially if they know they overreacted. If you hide under a rock and do not openly address the situation with the customer, you will not be respected. If you do not regain your respect, the customer will likely come back and repeat the same disrespect over and over, and it may actually worsen.

You can avoid these situations in the future by utilizing one essential tool: communication. Communication between the consultant and the customer on a daily basis will go a long way to minimize those unwanted surprises that can cause problems between the two participants.

PART 1: WORKING WITH CLIENTS

3. Pick Up the Phone and Talk to the Client the Old-Fashioned Way

We live in a world that has so many different ways to communicate. The means of communicating through voice, video, and data seem endless—and the possibilities are all changing at such a rapid pace that it makes it difficult to keep up! It's fun to try, though. Many people love tinkering with electronic toys and spend countless hours learning how they work.

Email is one of the most popular ways to communicate among people in business transactions. Some people prefer using email as their primary or only way to communicate in business. Obviously, email is an efficient and effective means of communicating and has several positive benefits, but it also has some negative aspects. Composing emails takes more time than leaving a client a voicemail or conducting a phone conversation. Additionally, many people compose emails that are not well written and this hurts their professional credibility.

I don't know about you, but I never write something perfect the first time and in order to send an email that is professional I need to rewrite it (or at least carefully read through it) a couple of times. However, I find that a voicemail or phone conversation is simple to communicate because it is much easier for me to talk than to write. I think that's true for most people. Email or voicemail is like a curtain that creates a lining or filter between real time communication. This lining effect can be beneficial in one sense in that we can control our days better and communicate swiftly, but it can also be detrimental, such as using it to screen calls and avoid real time communication.

CONSULTANT, CONSULT!

I believe the best way in which a consultant can communicate to a client is through the old-fashioned act of picking up the phone. A phone conversation gives you as the consultant an opportunity to display your personality and competency to the client. The more the client knows about you from a professional perspective, the more you will establish a stronger professional relationship. The client will be in a position to better understand the thinking and strategy you are using to solve their problems. If phone conversations are conducted properly, then you will develop tremendous professional respect from the client.

Personally, I am not a big fan of spending personal time with clients, other than taking in a sporting event from time to time. Many consultants have ruined their professional relationship with clients by establishing too much of a personal relationship. For example, the consultant may drink too much alcohol at some personal function and this could be offensive to a client and result in a loss of respect for the consultant. Instead, just pick up the phone—and keep the conversation primarily on business matters!

I personally assume that if a consultant is hesitant in picking up the phone to talk with a client, then they probably lack the confidence and character that is necessary in the consulting business or in any business for that matter.

In my business career, I have seen some consultants simply refuse to pick up the phone and talk to clients, especially to give them ideas that could result in future work. My experience has taught me that a consultant's inability to do this will make it difficult for them to rise upward in the organization they work for.

PART I: WORKING WITH CLIENTS

4
Know How to Scope a Job

Scoping a job refers to the manner in which a consultant identifies the budget and tasks that are necessary to properly perform the job. Clients have their own ideas as to how much something should cost and what it takes to complete a job. But you will need to establish a fair and reasonable fee for your services.

Before a consultant can realistically establish a budget and determine the steps necessary to complete the job, they must understand the client's needs. The client may ask the consultant to perform an extensive financial analysis but may want to pay only a minor amount for this service. In this case, the consultant should (a) explain to the client that performing the type of service requested requires a larger budget or (b) describe the type of work product that could be provided given the client's budget expectations. Obviously, the later approach would require the consultant to perform much less analysis, which may or may not meet the client's needs.

Determining the client's purpose and need for the consultant's information can help both parties scope the job. If the client wants the information in order to make a broad brush, big picture decision about doing or not doing something, the lesser scope and budget may be adequate. If the client wants the information to go borrow money or attract a joint venture partner, however, then the larger scope and budget would likely be more appropriate. I have been involved in client engagements where the client initially agrees to the lesser scope and lower budget, but then as the job progresses the client significantly expands the scope of work. In this case, it is the consultant's responsibility to re-communicate with the client about expanding the budget.

CONSULTANT, CONSULT!

Whenever possible, the initial client engagement letter should spell out the procedures for making changes to the scope of work. Such changes should be approved in writing with signatures from both parties. Never start doing more work without that client's signature on the contract addendum, unless you have been told to start and you're willing to take a possible non-payment risk.

Attempt to find ways to be of service to the client, but also realize that the quality and professionalism of your work must never be compromised. There may be services you simply cannot agree to perform for the client because the client is willing to pay only a certain amount. Always maintain quality and professionalism in the marketplace. Never compromise your standards in an attempt to appease a client's demands.

How many times have you seen another consultant's work get bashed because it lacked quality and professionalism? In my business, I see it happen all the time. Back in the 1980s there was a nationally recognized CPA firm called Leventhol & Horwath that ranked among the top 10 big accounting firms in the United States. The firm offered many different consulting services, including the preparation of hotel feasibility studies that they charged clients an average of $5,000 to perform. Leventhol & Horwath ended up getting sued over many of these feasibility studies, and because of this and other things, the partnership dissolved. Many believe the partners of the firm failed to make sure the services could be properly done for the price and in a manner that would maintain quality and professionalism.

Upper management and consultants must take the necessary time to properly scope client jobs to ensure your consulting firm's success and your client's satisfaction over the long haul.

PART I: WORKING WITH CLIENTS

Always Prepare for Client Meetings

Most of the client meetings I go to cost the client a lot of money so it behooves the consultant to be properly prepared. Clients appreciate the consultant who comes prepared to meetings. In fact, if you don't come prepared, you probably will not be invited back. It's not enough to physically show up to a meeting with nothing in hand. Sometimes, I just have to laugh (and cringe) inside when I see someone show up to a meeting appearing as though their major accomplishment of the day was to make the meeting on time.

You should always bring an agenda and any appurtenant analysis to a client meeting regardless of whether it is an internal client meeting or a meeting with a large group that includes other people. By doing this, you are controlling or influencing the conclusions that will be reached at the end of the meeting. The information presented should clearly describe the goals of the client.

In my experience, an agenda by itself is not enough unless it's fairly detailed because I find meeting participants will tend to generalize their comments and conversation. Accompanying detailed analysis supporting agenda discussion points is useful because it forces the group to focus more specifically on the topic. A substantive discussion of the topic will allow the consultant to pin down the meeting participants into making decisions or find specifically where the parties may disagree on an issue.

It's the consultant's job to push the agenda to achieve meaningful results or conclusions that are credible and professional at the fastest rate possible for the client's benefit. How many times have you gone to a meeting where it is apparent that none of the parties at the table feel any sense of urgency?

CONSULTANT, CONSULT!

How many times have you gone to a series of meetings where they keep talking about the same topics or issues but the parties fail to reach any conclusions? Obviously, meetings that are conducted in this manner indicate the participants lack care or concern for the client's wallet. In fact, I have seen some meeting participants utilize delaying tactics as their mode of operation so that they can make more money or create greater job security. At the end of the day, however, the client always knows who is effective in getting results from meetings and those participants that did not contribute in a meaningful way will likely not be attending future meetings.

The consultant who provides productive meeting results will find themselves getting more and more work from the client, and this is one of the ways the consultant ensures their future job growth and security.

There are several things you can do in advance of a meeting to ensure it is effective and productive. I like to talk individually with key decision-makers in advance if possible. Discussions on an individualized basis are extremely useful because I find people are much more relaxed and this creates an environment for a meaningful discussion of the issues.

If feasible, I will attempt to reach an agreement with the key decision-makers before the meeting so that when the meeting actually takes place the script is already set and the meeting becomes more of a role playing disclosure formality to the group of participants. This approach is used in the spirit of getting quicker meeting results and is not intended to circumvent the benefits that can occur from the participation of all meeting participants.

Another thing a consultant can do is to make sure all necessary research and analysis that will be useful for the meeting is completed and circulated prior to the meeting. The distribution of this information indicates that parties should be prepared to discuss pertinent

PART I: WORKING WITH CLIENTS

information at the meeting. If this information is not circulated in advance and instead distributed at the meeting, participants will likely say that they need time to review and will discuss it at the next meeting. This definitely delays the goal of timely completion.

One last note: It is a cardinal sin to show up late to a meeting. Clients despise tardiness and if you show up late you will have a difficult time trying to gain control of the meeting.

Be Confident with a Client and Rely on Firm Resources

Crossing the bridge from college into the working world is a difficult and sometimes painful transition. Everything is new and different. An individual is faced with a double whammy: learn the protocol of working in an office and learn how to be productive for the company and the client. Most companies don't expect new hires from college to know much because they have little truly relevant work experience. The company is usually relying on the reputation of the college attended and the personal characteristics of the person when making their decision to hire. Once the individual is hired, the company will attempt to train and groom them in a manner consistent with the company's philosophy.

Because of this reality, new hires are susceptible to showing signs of insecurity in front of a client due to their lack of experience. Many companies keep recent college graduates in the back office for a while to gain some experience before sending them out to talk and work directly for clients. Some companies keep the recent college graduates in the back office too long, however, to the detriment of their personal career path.

CONSULTANT, CONSULT!

My opinion is that you must get the recent college graduate in front of the client at the earliest practical time. Getting in front of the client is one of the best ways to help a recent college graduate develop confidence and achieve a real sense of job fulfillment.

When the recent college graduate begins to interact with the client, he or she needs to prepare properly so they can be as confident as possible in front of the client. If a client gets a sense that the new consultant may not know what they are doing, or if they are too tentative in their communications, the client may call a senior person in your company to ask for someone else. In order to avoid this happening, a prudent company will make sure the new consultant is properly prepared by giving them examples of relevant work product and/or by having detailed discussions with the new consultant prior to sending them out to interact with their first client(s).

The moral of the story? Coach recent college graduates to not act insecure with the client and not freely admit they lack work experience, and this is primarily achieved by proper job preparation. Of course, if the client asks about relevant work experience, they should receive an honest answer. Then again, they also should be informed that if an issue or topic comes up that the young consultant is not able to handle personally, they can and will discuss it with the senior management in their company.

A senior manager should take the necessary amount of time with the young consultant to make sure the issue or topic is fully understood so that an accurate answer can be provided to the client. Just so everyone is on the same page, the senior manager and young consultant should call the client together to discuss the issue or topic to make sure the client is fully satisfied with the answer given. The client will typically be satisfied as long as the resources in your company are used in a timely manner to resolve their issues.

PART I: WORKING WITH CLIENTS

If too much time passes between when the client raises the issue or topic with the young consultant and when the senior manager and young consultant provide the client with the answers, you run the risk of upsetting the client. If the young consultant is not getting the proper attention to secure an answer to the client's question, then he or she should express their concerns to another senior manager in the company. The young consultant, after all, is the one who has an obligation to respond to the client in a timely manner.

When the young consultant is doing a good job and solving problems, their confidence and experience will grow naturally. Most clients understand that many things we do may be done for the first time. As long as the young consultant is doing a good job, it's unlikely they will have any qualms.

The new consultant needs to remember he or she is representing the consulting firm. The whole weight of the company—decades or centuries of accumulated experience—is at his or her disposal. A prudent young consultant will fully leverage this accumulated experience to accelerate his or her professional growth and development. In that sense, while the new consultant isn't an expert yet, the company is. And the company is fully committed to passing along its expertise to him or her.

Any smart college graduate can learn what it takes to become an expert in his or her own right. That expertise comes from the young consultant's personal professional experience—one client at a time, starting from year one, while fully leveraging the accumulated experience of others in his or her firm.

CONSULTANT, CONSULT!

7
Referrals from Existing Clients Are the Key to Success

Some companies operate their business by cold calling on prospective customers. A great example of this is the telemarketing business. I don't know about you, but I am not excited to talk to a telemarketer about anything after a long day of work. Obviously, this approach to business requires voluminous calls before you secure a sale with a customer. Significant time and energy is invested in the cold calling process and one has to always question the cost effectiveness of this approach. A prudent business will deploy its human resources in the most cost effective way to achieve the best revenue producing results for the company.

In the professional consulting business, the most cost effective way of succeeding and growing the business is to obtain referrals from existing clients. Clearly, this requires that you do excellent work to gain referrals. Most prudent clients that you have met for the first time will give you only one job to work on. In their mind, it is a test to see how well you perform. If you pass the test, they will usually open up a larger book of jobs for you.

Be sure to share this accomplishment with the upper management in your company. It's encouraging for everyone in a company to see the personal growth and internal confidence a consultant develops when he or she succeeds in getting more client work or a referral. They can see the excitement in your eyes from knowing that you are on the right path for upward movement within the company.

It's important to note that simply selling the job is not enough to secure more work and referrals. You must do the job and do it well by producing tangible results. In fact, the only way a prudent consultant sells more work and gets more referrals is by first doing an excellent job on the client's work.

Additionally, you should always invest time with your clients to understand all the other projects underway at their company. Conversations like this can open the door for you to tell the client that you also have good job experience in some of the other areas that the client is focusing on as well. These conversations can be a great opportunity for you to let the client know that you would be interested in helping on these additional projects. It helps if you have some insights or words of caution for the client regarding other areas of their business.

I tell consultants that a performance review from the management within your company is important, but it's much more important to get a good evaluation from your client. This is manifested by the client giving you more work and referring you to similar companies. Just imagine how fast a company could grow if the vast majority of its consultants obtained more work from existing clients as well as referrals. This would certainly buck the trend of most companies that operate on a 20/80 principle in that 20 percent of the workforce creates 80 percent of the firm's productivity. If you are not getting more work from existing clients, then you are not doing a good enough job for your client.

Consultants can provide every excuse in the book as to why they are not getting more work from existing clients, but none of these excuses are acceptable long-term. Clients are the best judge of your abilities or lack thereof. Upper management needs to monitor and be aware of each consultant's successes or failures and attempt to coach the consultants that are not achieving this goal. The company simply will not survive and grow if it retains underachieving consultants and fails to secure client referrals.

CONSULTANT, CONSULT!

- 8 -
Take Client Bills Personally

In business, there are many employees who fail to make the connection between the dollars billed to a client and the work being performed. This is especially true on larger jobs where the budget is big and many people are working together. Some companies fail to properly review bills before they go out to a client.

At my company, there is a partner-level review and a quality-control review of the bills before they go out to the client. Some of the questions we ask ourselves when reviewing the bills are: Would I personally pay this bill if it was sent to me? Is the employee's time charged to the correct job? Is the time charged to the job representative of the work performed? Is this bill reasonable?
If you cannot answer yes to the questions, you may want to consider revising or adjusting the bill based on particular facts and circumstances. One of the quickest ways of upsetting a client is to send them a bill that doesn't properly reconcile with their expectations of the work being performed on their behalf.

Typical billing adjustments consist of holding time or cutting time. Holding time refers to the notion that the time charges are good, but it's more appropriate to bill the client for this time at a later date that more appropriately matches when the client will realize the benefit of the services provided. Cutting time refers to the notion that the time charges are not representative of the company's professional standard and the company is unwilling to allow this time to be charged to the client. Obviously, if you have an employee who has his or her time charges being cut on a consistent basis, then that employee is not being reasonably productive in his or her job. The company must focus on this individual and coach him or

PART I: WORKING WITH CLIENTS

her to improve. If improvement does not occur, the company will have no choice but to counsel them out of the business.

A smart company will set competitive billing rates. In the consulting business, there are many companies that charge excessive hourly rates to their clients. Companies with high-priced billing rates spend significant amounts of time arguing with their clients over bills, and many times only 50 percent of the bill is actually paid and the balance of time is cut. One has to question the long-term merit of this approach, because it seems to indicate a tremendous imbalance between the dollars charged to the client and value of the services provided to the client. I think this is a terrible business approach that fails in the long run, and it certainly doesn't help foster trust between client and consulting firm.

In the retail business, Wal-Mart is a great example of providing good products for a great price. They have replicated their business model all over the United States with tremendous success because they simply provide the best price to the consumer buying their products.

Now I realize that there are some clients that make it their regular business practice to automatically complain about bills because they believe some companies will bow down to the pressure and discount the bill. Of course, most companies will figure out which clients deploy this approach toward billings. The bottom line is that if you believe your company's billing is fair and reasonable, you should expect the client to pay the bill. Listen attentively to their concerns, but hold steadfast if the bill is reasonable. If the client isn't happy that you didn't adjust a reasonable bill, they may stop using the services of your company, but this may be an appropriate result.

Don't get me wrong: I don't ever want to lose a client, but if a client is not willing to pay the bill for services rendered that are reasonable, you're just wasting your time by working with the client.

9 Take Client Budgets Seriously

Setting a proper budget for a job that you're preparing to work on for a client is an important task. Every company that's providing a service for another company should be expected to establish a budget no matter how difficult this may be. The accounting department within the company seeking services needs to include the job in its accounting system so that payments can be made as the job progresses. The budget is also used to initiate the job in the system. It's important to reach a specific understanding with the client about the budget you are setting for their job. Before you can really establish a meaningful budget, the scope and approach on the job must be determined. Then the budget can be determined based on this information.

Two types of budgets are typically used in the services business—a time and material budget not to exceed a specified amount without the approval of the client, and a fixed price budget. Time and material budgets are estimates and can be revised if necessary to complete the job, if the client is amenable to this. A budget based on time and material is appropriate when the employee performing the work doesn't have complete control of the process necessary to complete the job. A consultant working on a job that requires interaction and negotiation with 10 other consultants is a good example of when a time and material budget is appropriate.

A fixed price budget means the employee must finish the job for a fixed amount of money no matter how much time and resources are needed to complete the job. A budget based on a fixed price is appropriate when the employee performing the work has everything necessary to complete the job within their control. For

PART I: WORKING WITH CLIENTS

example, a painter setting a price for painting a house is a good example of when a fixed price budget could be used.

My company prepares an engagement letter that describes the relevant background or job setting, the objectives of the job, the scope and approach of the job, and the timing and budget of the job. Enough time should be spent preparing the engagement letter so that it demonstrates that care and concern has been put into its preparation. A good engagement letter also serves as a work plan for those performing the service for the client. When you commence a job that's an hourly bill rate time and material structure, you should have a monitoring system in place to understand the time and dollars that are being charged to the job. These dollars should be compared to the budget so you can gauge how you are doing relative to the budget.

If the actual dollars incurred on the job are beginning to come close to the time and material budget and you realize you will most likely exceed the budget, you should call the client and inform them of this, as a matter of courtesy and, usually, as a contractual requirement, so that the client can determine how to deal with the situation.

The majority of clients will ask for an addendum letter that describes why the company is requesting a larger budget to complete the job. The company should carefully describe the reasons for going over budget for the client's review. Typical reasons would relate to events or situations that were not anticipated when the budget was originally set. For example, perhaps the engagement took five revisions instead of two. Obviously, more revisions to an engagement will drive up the costs on the job.

Most clients don't want you to stop midstream in their work because a partially complete work product has little value to them, so they will usually approve the addendum letters and modify the contract. A small portion of clients may ask you to stop work so they can attempt to finish the work themselves.

Clients Do Review Their Bills

It is important for companies that bill hours for client jobs to carefully and accurately prepare the billing invoices. One of the quickest ways of losing the client's trust and confidence is by submitting them a billing invoice that is unprofessional and careless.

Never make the assumption that your client will simply rubber stamp the approval of your billing invoice because, the fact is, they carefully review the bill and compare it to their perception and understanding of what they think you are doing on their job. Many employees in the services business grumble about having to account for their time and allocate it to the jobs they're working on for their clients. Yes, it's a painful, tedious process but it's a necessary evil of the business and you must get over the grumbling. Always take whatever time is necessary to properly make sure billing invoices to clients are well done, without exceptions.

The descriptions written on a billing invoice should be clear and concise. Sometimes employees do not provide enough written detail on the billing invoice and the client is not able to understand what the employee purported to do on the job. Other times employees provide too much detail on the billing invoice and the client becomes bogged down trying to understand what the employee did on the job. Both of these examples may result in the client having to pick up the phone and dialogue to better understand what the employee purported to do on the job.

PART I: WORKING WITH CLIENTS

If the client has to make a call on the billing invoice, then the billing invoice is insufficient and the employees working on the job should get a clue that they need to improve future billings. The actual time spent on the job should be allocated to the job—nothing more or nothing less. The actual time spent on the job should be timely billed to a client, and not several months later when they have forgotten what you did for them. The timing of the work product provided to the client should closely correspond to the timing of the client's receipt of the billing invoice because information related to the work will be fresh in the client's mind.

The employee should not personally cut his or her time because upper management of the company needs to know how much time certain jobs actually take to complete in terms of time and dollars. It is upper management's responsibility to determine if time should be cut from a job, not the employee's. Upper management needs to know about actual time incurred on jobs because this factors back into the budget-setting process for future jobs.

If the employee has any doubts about charging his or her time to a client related to a particular service, the employee should ask upper management how they want to handle this relative to the billing invoice process. Admittedly, there are certain work functions that oftentimes are not appropriate to bill to a client. These functions typically relate to marketing or administrative matters. For example, if a client wants you to come to their office for an initial marketing meeting you need to determine, upfront before you go, if you are going to charge them for your time. If the client is not willing to pay for the meeting time, then you may want to suggest to them that you would like to have them come to your office for the meeting so as to minimize the free time involved and remove any travel time and cost from the equation.

CONSULTANT, CONSULT!

Of course, each client opportunity is different. There may be times—because of the size of the job opportunity—that you will go to the client's office for a free initial meeting. This thinking will change with the good or bad economics in the marketplace, in that, in a bad marketplace you probably will give clients more free initial meetings than you would in a good marketplace.

When Is a Job Sold and When Should You Start Working on It?

In the services business, it is sometimes difficult to understand when to start working on a client's job that you believe you have sold. Sometimes a consultant believes they are engaged by the client and they spend time processing the job only to find out several weeks later—usually after the client receives the first billing invoice—that the client did not have the same understanding and is unwilling to pay the invoice. Obviously, this is not a good situation for anybody to be in. The key to avoiding these situations is to make sure you have a clear understanding with the client upfront, usually at the initial meeting, if possible.

One of the things I do at the initial meeting is to ask the client if they want us to immediately get started on the job or if they want us to wait until we have entered into a contract with them. Because it can take several weeks to secure a contract, most clients (assuming a reasonable economy is in place) may ask you to get going immediately with the understanding of the tentative budget for the job. If the client says they want us to get going on the job at the initial meeting, I will usually follow up that day or the next day with an email confirming the client's directions.

PART I: WORKING WITH CLIENTS

Though the client may want you to get going on the job, you still have an obligation to your company to appropriately size up the reputation of the client. For example, is the client a new client or an existing client? Does the client have any invoice payment history with the company? What do other consultants or attorneys that may have worked with the client in the past have to say about working with this client, including their invoice payment experiences? Is the new client a big or small company? How did you feel about the client in your initial meeting?

If the answers to these questions are positive, then you should get going on the job. If the answers are somewhat negative, you may want to wait until you have a signed contract for the job. If the feedback is fairly negative, you will need to seriously consider whether you should even begin working with the new client. If the client is new to the company and you are unable to obtain information from others about this client, you may want to consider getting a retainer before actually starting the job.

As a matter of practice in the real estate industry, if the client has asked you to start working on a job ahead of having an approved contract, they have a moral obligation, and perhaps a legal obligation, to pay your invoice. Most clients will honor this obligation, but there are some who may change their mind, so it's crucial for you to evaluate the client as discussed above.

In one meeting, a client asked us to begin working on his job and also asked if we could expedite his project ahead of other projects we were working on in the office. We agreed to get going on the job, confirmed this via email, and gave him the priority he asked for because I had worked with this client six years earlier without difficulty. Unfortunately, this time was a different experience. The employees in my office worked two weeks on the job and the client got his first billing invoice. The client called and said the he thought we were doing this work for him as a part of our non-chargeable marketing costs and was unwilling to pay the invoice. I explained to him that we had started the job at his request, and I reminded him that we were unable to complete the project for free. We immediately stopped all work on the job and terminated our relationship with this company.

You can always do things right, but that doesn't guarantee that others will. If you determine it is appropriate to wait until you have obtained an approved contract to perform the work, you are assured that you have a legal contract that is fully enforceable if the client decides to change their mind about paying the invoices on the job. Obviously, you must use good judgment in evaluating the client, because no consultant wants to end up working for free.

What Should Be in a Client Engagement Letter?

Usually after meeting with a prospective client, the client will ask you to provide an engagement letter that describes the salient things you plan to do on the job. The purpose of the engagement letter from the consultant's perspective is to demonstrate that you have a clear understanding of what needs to be done on the job at hand. It's extremely important to present a prospective client with an engagement letter demonstrating professionalism and substance of thought and ideas. Fancy and colorful engagement letters that lack substance usually fail to impress a sophisticated client.

You must also be mindful of the prospective client's motives relative to an engagement letter. Some prospective clients already have someone else in mind to use on the job and may only be asking

PART I: WORKING WITH CLIENTS

you to provide an engagement letter so that they can stuff it in their file and satisfy their company's policy of obtaining multiple bids on a prospective job. There are questions you can ask at the initial meeting to try to flush out this possibility so that you don't waste time with a client who has no intention of hiring you for the job.

Another thing you should avoid is giving too much detail in an engagement letter. That way, if the client decides not to use you, they don't end up with a detailed work plan that they can give to another consultant they are planning to use on the prospective job. The majority of clients that ask for engagement letters, however, will end up hiring you for the prospective job.

Most of the clients that hire a consulting company use their own contracts and usually attach all or a portion of the consulting company's engagement letter as an exhibit to the contract. It is extremely important that you review the contract in detail and make sure it isn't saying something contrary to the consultant's engagement letter. If there are any discrepancies, be sure to revise the client's contract. Submit two versions: one with all changes tracked and another with all changes accepted. In a cover letter, ask the potential client to review all of the changes and inform you if they want to add, delete, or make any other changes. Otherwise, if it looks fine, ask them to print out two copies, sign them, and mail both to you. Countersign both and mail one back to the client.

A sound engagement letter will contain sections on background, scope and approach, information needed from the client, timing, and budget. The background section should clearly state the relevant facts about the prospective job, and it should also explain the situation that requires the assistance of the consultant's relevant experience. Enough should be written so that the client is confident that you understand the situation you're being asked to deal with. This information will also be useful for any other consultants in your company who may also work on the job.

CONSULTANT, CONSULT!

The scope and approach section should identify the specific tasks you plan to perform and achieve relative to the prospective job. This section should contain enough detail so that others in your company will understand the necessary steps to properly complete the prospective job. Often a detailed work plan may be written for internal use by the consultants working on the prospective job. However, it is usually wise not to provide this detailed plan in the engagement letter, as mentioned earlier.

The section regarding information needed from the client should be straightforward and simple for the client to assemble. You don't want to appear as though you're giving the client homework because, after all, that's why they're hiring you.

The timing and budget section should identify a timeframe for completing and finishing the job and its estimated cost. If a client insists on having a tight timeframe to finish the job, you should make sure that the time clock starts after you have received all the information necessary to start the job. For example, you could agree to produce a first draft of the work two weeks after you receive all of the information from the client. If the client hasn't provided the information, you will need to remind the client that the two-week timeframe has not commenced.

The budget amount needs to be a realistic expectation of what the prospective job will cost to perform given the professional standards of your consulting company. A budget set too low can upset the client if actual costs end up exceeding the budget, and a budget set too high may prevent you from even getting the job because the client views it as too expensive. At my consulting company, many of our jobs are time and material based jobs since we are unable to fully control the outcome on most of the jobs we work on. If you can control all of the factors involved in the cost of the project, however, you may want to use a fixed fee bid.

PART I: WORKING WITH CLIENTS

Some Other Not So Obvious Ways of Selling Client Services

This book has already touched on some of the traditional means that companies use to sell the services they have to offer, but there are many other not so obvious ways of selling work that can produce tangible results. Obviously, simply picking up the phone and cold calling prospective clients is one way of selling your company's services, but in order for this to be successful you need to have someone who is effective on the phone, and unfortunately most professionals are not very comfortable doing this.

The email traffic in business is huge in terms of its use and this provides an excellent avenue for communicating with clients about the possibility of doing more work for them. It seems like email usage in business is more prevalent than voicemail these days. One not so obvious way of selling business is to send a periodic email to clients giving them information that is relevant to their companies and the projects they customarily work on.

In the real estate business, you may be aware that a municipality recently increased its development impact fees. A simple electronic postcard that gives clients information of which they may not be aware is a great way of showing that you're always thinking about them and their project. My company does this on a regular basis. We often send out a postcard to hundreds of clients and end up getting one or two new jobs from the mailing. This gives us the perfect opportunity to discuss other services that the firm provides as well.

Another not so obvious way of selling business, especially for markets and clients that are new to your company, is to send an electronic postcard to the existing clients who also operate in the new market. The postcard would announce that your company has opened a new office in the new marketplace, succinctly describe the services your company offers, provide a click-through to your company Website for more information, and attach a list of your company's previous jobs for the client, with contact information so that they can review and call for references. The postcard will also identify one or two specific services that your company is planning to initially focus on based on the preliminary research that was done in this new market area. These one or two service areas should be identified as some of the most needed services in the new market area. This electronic postcard is an excellent example of working the referral system from your company's existing book of business.

Another not so obvious way of selling new business is to develop an electronic postcard that allows prospective clients to see the actual results that your company may achieve as a result of its services. For example, my company has an excellent track record of representing the building industry in negotiating positive adjustments to development impact fee studies on behalf of our clients. Oftentimes, this work and the results make it into the newspaper or other published sources. Our postcard to prospective clients would indicate that we achieved another successful result for the building industry, and it would provide links to these past publications so that the prospective client can read for themselves and understand the actual results achieved by our company.

Of course, the postcard would state that if the prospective client is faced with a similar issue, such as the one identified on the postcard, we would be happy to discuss with them how we could be of service. This type of postcard is extremely powerful because it describes real-world results your company has achieved, as opposed to describing what your company might be able to achieve with a particular service.

PART I: WORKING WITH CLIENTS

Electronic postcards are a good example of push technology via the Internet. A postcard is succinct and is placed on a silver platter for the prospective client to review at their convenience without the pressure of having someone sitting across the table or on the phone trying to compel them to make a decision. In order to complete the selling process with electronic postcards, it is important to follow up with a phone call to the prospective clients who viewed the postcard. Software technology exists that allows you to see which prospective clients opened the email, and it also allows you to see if they clicked on and opened the links provided.

14. Watch Out for Contract Snafus

After an initial meeting with a prospective client, the consultant sends the client an engagement letter that describes the services the consultant plans to perform for the client. Notwithstanding the consultant's engagement letter, a vast majority of clients have their own consulting services contract they want the consulting company to sign and execute.

A prudent consultant and consulting company will carefully read each provision of the client's contract because there can be provisions in the contract that the consulting company may not or should not agree to. There are seven major areas to watch for:

1. If you are a consulting firm that works on a time and material basis, you should carefully confirm this is what the contract says because I have seen many contracts that attempt to establish a fixed price contract and a requirement that commits the consultant to perform the hours necessary to finish the job even if it costs more than the fixed price.

CONSULTANT, CONSULT!

The company I work for rarely does a fixed price contract because we don't have complete control over the jobs we work on for our clients. You may talk to the client, and the client may assure you that the contract is a time and material contract, but it really doesn't matter what the client says. All that matters is what the contract says. You must read the contract in its entirety because oftentimes contracts have time and material language in one area and fixed price language in another area.

2. Another contract provision may require the consulting company to pay the client if the consulting company doesn't complete the job within a specified timeframe. Obviously, most consulting companies could never agree to such a ludicrous provision because again, they don't have complete control of the job they're working on.

3. Another area to watch out for is insurance requirements. Some companies seek high limits that are above and beyond the industry standard or they require certain insurance company ratings that are not achievable in the marketplace. Indemnification provisions can also get out of hand and most reasonable provisions cut both ways for the parties in the contract and not just one way conveniently to the client's benefit.

4. Be on the watch for clients' contracts that attempt to lock in your hourly billing rates for the duration of the job, which can extend over a long period of time. Most consulting companies adjust their billing rates on an annual basis and contracts that lock in billing rates can frustrate the economics of the consulting company, especially if the company has a few large jobs.

5. Watch carefully the scope of work that has been identified in the contract. I have seen clients include the scope of work from the engagement letter that was provided to them from the consulting company, but also include additional scope of work that the con-

sulting company did not anticipate doing when it set its budget in the engagement letter.

6. Carefully review the termination provisions of the contract and make sure they are reasonable. Most provisions in this area state that the client can stop the consultant's work at any time for any reason after giving proper notice. This provision seems fair, but make sure there are no punitive provisions attached to it. Oftentimes, the client's contract will state that the work product is to be turned over to the client as their property and many of the consulting company's tools are proprietary, so make sure these tools or models are not included in this provision.

7. Lastly, most client contracts include confidentiality provisions, so be mindful of these provisions, especially when talking to other clients about your client's job.

Why Do Clients Hire Consultants?

There are a multitude of reasons why a company hires an outside consulting company. It's important for the consulting company and its consultants to understand the client's rationale for hiring them so the company can make the necessary adjustments to fully exploit client opportunities. Of course, there are times where the consulting company needs to simply advise the client to hire them for a specific service if the service is something you know they need. These are the top five reasons for clients to use the services of a consultant:

1. Clients sometimes hire outside consulting companies to perform work because they don't have the internal labor resources to get the job done within the timeframe needed. Consulting companies

usually have the ability to juggle things around in order to satisfy the time requirements of the client. I remember a client who would call on Thursdays or Fridays and give our company an assignment that he wanted by the next Monday or Tuesday. After meeting with him and talking to him enough times after the assignments were completed and delivered, I figured out that he was using us primarily because he didn't want work to mess up his Friday afternoon of golf or his weekend.

2. Another reason clients hire outside consulting companies is due to the fact that most consulting companies have greater experience at doing the job than the client does. If the consulting company has performed over 100 assignments that are similar to the relevant assignment, and the client has only dealt with the issue a couple of times, it is likely that the consulting company will be able to do a much better job on the assignment than the client would.

In one meeting, a client thought he had mastered a particular service I was more familiar with and experienced in. He decided to implement that particular service by himself without my or anyone else's assistance. Years later, I was hired by a new owner who displaced my former client because of bad management of the project. I had a chance to review the particular service the prior owner/client had confined to a legal agreement, only to find that he "gave away the farm" because of his inexperience. This mistake alone cost the project millions of dollars.

3. Clients also use consulting companies that have a solid industry reputation in certain service areas because they need to demonstrate to others, such as a financial partner, that they are using the best resource in the marketplace to get the job done.

4. Another common reason clients use consulting companies is due to internal second-guessing. They know that most consulting

PART I: WORKING WITH CLIENTS

companies have lots of brain power and intellect, and they often want to tap into it as a way of confirming ideas or decisions. A smart consulting company will rise to the occasion when a client gives them an opportunity to review and improve an analysis.

5. Clients have a tendency to use outside consultants in tougher economic times so they can reduce internal labor costs and have greater flexibility in deciding where they need to expend resources relative to ongoing operations. The prudent client will seek and use the services of a consulting company that always offers a net financial benefit opportunity to the client's bottom line.

What Does Your Client Think about You?

One of the best forms of consultant evaluation in business comes directly from the clients the consultant serves. The consultant normally obtains a continuous flow of client feedback on jobs. One hopes most of the feedback is positive, but there are times when it's not. A consultant should consider the feedback as an ongoing evaluation process, and this should be considered more important than the evaluation process the consultant goes through within his or her own company. The feedback the client provides often is the most objective information relating to job performance, while employee evaluations from within the company can sometimes lack objectivity.

Consultant/client relationships are usually all business. A sign that the consultant has received negative feedback from the client can be a consultant referring to the client in a negative way when speaking to co-workers. Sometimes the truth hurts and most individuals are not quick to admit they did something wrong. However, if the client's feedback is credible and objective, the consultant should learn from his or her mistakes and take immediate corrective actions.

Among other things, the consultant must become a good listener to client needs and expectations. At the end of the day, if you want to stay in business, you must make sure that the client thinks nothing but positive things about your performance on their job. If you want to live in denial about what your client may be saying to you—or about you to others—you most certainly will fail to get more work from this client, as well as any referrals you might otherwise have obtained. In fact, things can actually get worse for you if clients tell other prospective clients about your shortcomings, especially if the client has decided to no longer use your services. This situation has another ripple effect relative to the consulting company. When upper management finds out that the client has severed relationships because of a particular consultant's lack of performance, the consultant's job security may be at risk, especially if it happens on more than one occasion.

It's important that the consultant understand what clients complain about most to avoid these situations. One of the biggest client complaints is that the employee is not getting their job done on time. From the get go, be extra careful to understand the client's deadlines and carefully evaluate what you need to do to reach their benchmarks.

Another typical complaint is that the consultant is not returning phone calls on a timely basis. You have a cell phone, office phone, and probably a home phone, too. Use one of them as soon as possible to return your client's call, even if it's after hours and you can leave only a voice mail message.

A consultant showing up late to meetings is another common complaint issued by clients. Be ready a day or two ahead of time. Don't

PART I: WORKING WITH CLIENTS

try to squeeze in one more thing before heading to your client's office. If in doubt, use Google or your GPS unit so you don't get lost. Strive to show up 20 minutes early. The extra time to mentally gear up is much better than coming in out of breath.

Clients also get upset when a consultant comes to a meeting unprepared and then attempts to take control of the meeting. Confirm both the agenda and meeting leadership plan 24 hours ahead of time. Ideally, listen first, and then talk.

If the consultant fails to inform his or her client of an issue relevant to the project, the client may begin to wonder if they need the consultant at all. Don't withhold important information, especially if it's not positive news. If you have good news, share that fact ASAP—even if you want to present the details later that same day in writing or in person.

If the client calls the consultant when they have tough issues to deal with, this is a great compliment to the consultant's capabilities. If the client asks the consultant to go to a baseball game, but never gives him or her any meaningful work, however, this is not a compliment. It may mean that the consultant and client have a relationship based on friendship, but they certainly don't have much of a business relationship. Then again, if the consultant can foster a client relationship that's based on both friendship and client-related work, the consultant will have a better chance of retaining this client long-term.

CONSULTANT, CONSULT!

PART 2
WORKING WITH A TEAM

CONSULTANT, CONSULT!

PART 2: WORKING WITH A TEAM

17 Watch Out When the Internal and External Views of a Person Are Radically Different

Have you ever met a person who believes the world cannot live without them? I remember giving an employee a written evaluation only to watch him go ballistic. He insisted the information outlined in that review was inaccurate. He was convinced he was doing a great job. Several people reviewed and contributed to the preparation of his evaluation, though, to enhance the objectivity of the evaluation. This was also not a first evaluation. He had worked with several senior consultants, all of whom had provided the same poor written evaluations and verbal feedback. This thorough approach to evaluating the underperforming employee ensured that I was not mistaken, and that any actions taken were justified.

What's the lesson for us all? For one, I believe it is extremely important to have a person work with several senior consultants so you can get diversified feedback regarding the consultant's performance. It is possible for a good employee to get a bad evaluation from a senior person who might feel threatened or envious of the employee. I had this happen to me one time in my career. I was fortunate enough to have other senior people around me who realized it was very unlikely for an employee to go from great or good to poor in a relatively short period of time.

Of course, if an employee was encountering significant personal issues or was faced with some life-changing event, then it is possible this transformation could occur over a relatively short period of time. Some personal issues, like a consultant dealing with a loved one's health crisis or death, need to be handled with care.

CONSULTANT, CONSULT!

Other issues, like a consultant struggling because of an online gambling addiction during office hours, may need to be addressed head-on in a direct, clear-cut manner (with proper documentation over a period of time should probation or dismissal become necessary).

Still, most issues simply come down to an employee who has a radically different view of themselves than do the rest of the people in the company. An essential key to being a good employee is to be accurate in your thinking, ideas, and opinions. No wonder Socrates, Thales, Lao-tzu, and other ancient philosophers, as well as Alexander Pope, Ralph Waldo Emerson, and other more recent sages have urged us to "Know yourself." That's sound advice in every sphere of life, not just business.

My experience is that if employees have unrealistic views of themselves, then they will almost always have some type of flaw in their thinking processes. Allowing this type of employee to continue to work is not healthy for the company or other employees. Unfortunately, an employee who is out of touch with reality is like a cancer; he or she must be removed for the benefit of all other company participants.

I cannot tell you how many sleepless nights I spent trying to figure out a way of helping this type of personality prosper in the work environment, but the sad fact is you will simply find yourself wasting time. In the end, it is a relief to let go of the employee with unrealistic views, and the balance of company employees will be equally relieved. Ironically, when you deliver the termination notice to this type of employee, he or she will insist they don't understand why they are being let go.

There are several specific signs you can observe to determine if an employee has different internal views of himself or herself relative to the external views of others. Do they fail to listen to others? Are they

PART 2: WORKING WITH A TEAM

generally negative no matter what the topic? Do they believe they are highly intelligent while those around them wonder how one could possibly believe what they say?

What's the verdict? Do you need to take steps to deal with this within your own company? Or do you need to modify your own behavior? Little errors of thinking can become huge problems later. For the good of everyone, take decisive action.

Be a Team Player, Not a Lone Star Cowboy or Cowgirl

I don't know if it's just my imagination, but it seems as though the younger generation of students coming from college seem to work better in teams than the older generation. Maybe it's due to organized sports that young kids participate in where teamwork is a major focus. Soccer organizations that emphasize teamwork have sprouted up across the United States over the last 30 years—as well as many other sporting associations. When I was a kid, the mainstream sport was primarily baseball, whereas football and basketball were primarily organized through the educational system. Additionally, the younger generation missed out on all the frills of the 1960s and 1970s, which seemed to have a theme focused on the individual.

I spent the early years of my career being a lone star cowboy, viewing myself as a hired gun. Over time, I began to realize that this approach is a tough road to hoe. You feel every bump and bruise along the ride. Don't get me wrong; I am not regretting the role I played, because the learning process and character that I accumulated have been memorable. I evolved and learned the importance of teamwork, and I would take a team over an individual anytime. A company should always monitor lone star consultants because sometimes they have a tendency to put themselves on a pedestal higher than others in the organization. This is counterproductive to the company and its employees, and the company should avoid this at all costs. Instead, the company should acknowledge the lone star consultant's contributions and pay them well.

The power of the team is unstoppable if properly structured. Each consultant on the team will have different strengths than others, and if each team member is fully deploying their strengths, the combined effect produces solid results for the client. One consultant might be a fabulous communicator and another may be extremely proficient in financial modeling. The two working in unison will produce better results for the client than one individual doing both tasks. It is equally important, however, to identify a consultant's weaknesses, and every attempt should be made by the team to assist the consultant in improving on such weaknesses.

Just being on a team with others that have such strengths will naturally improve the consultant's weaknesses through team interaction. It's always nice to have another team member to discuss the issues, problems, and ideas that you are dealing with. This intellectual volleying enhances and improves the solutions that you will provide your client.

A company will fail in the long run if its consultants don't interact well with each other. Teamwork with each other will accelerate the flow of knowledge within an organization, and this will cause the company to stand out ahead of its competition. There are times when you cannot be in two places at one time, and having a team where other members can fill in the holes is beneficial to the company and its clients.

PART 2: WORKING WITH A TEAM

It's also fun to have other team members who work together with the common interest of producing excellence in what they do.

19

Don't Work in a Vacuum

How often have you felt as if your decision making process was like a vacuum? Sales people are notorious for trying to limit your evaluation of service, compelling you to buy what they are selling. An interior designer will almost always give you one or two types of furniture choices to choose from when decorating your home. The designer intentionally limits the universe of alternatives because they believe the client will be confused and end up not making a decision to do something if too many choices are presented.

Some people are never capable of making a decision, so they are naturally comfortable with the designer's approach to decision making. Others are not comfortable with making a decision about something based on a narrow set of alternatives.

If time is on your side, you will undoubtedly be better served if you take the time to fully understand what you are getting into instead of just jumping blindly into something, especially if it is material. It's always good to think over a big decision.

Lots of people in business work in a vacuum and they don't even know it. They often take what is given to them as the gospel truth and fail to review it with a critical eye. They sometimes run out of time and release documents that they know they should have spent more time preparing or reviewing.

CONSULTANT, CONSULT!

A prudent consultant will always resist being put in a vacuum when preparing or reviewing their work. They know that working in a vacuum carries a high probability that mistakes will be made in their work and their professional reputation runs the risk of being tarnished.

The consultant also knows that if he or she does not have all the relevant facts surrounding their job they may reach the wrong conclusions or give bad advice to the client. A smart consultant will take the time needed to evaluate and execute the work at hand. If more time is necessary to obtain relevant information, then the consultant will figure out a way of getting this additional time to process the job.

If you find in your research of source documents references to other documents, you should continue to pursue these other references until fully reviewed. If you are reviewing an agreement, you must review it in its entirety, including exhibits and ancillary documents that describe the business points. How many times have you seen an agreement get circulated for comments without all the necessary attachments? Obviously, this happens much too often.

If you're in a client meeting and the other side is trying to leverage you to make a decision on the spot, it is prudent to ask if you can step outside with your client to discuss this matter privately. Once outside, you and your client should determine if you have considered all the relevant information on the topic that is being considered. If you both believe you have enough information to make a sound decision, a strategy should be formulated and you should re-enter the meeting and present your response.

If you don't believe you have enough information to make a sound decision, then you should re-enter the meeting and set a future meeting date to present a response after you have obtained the necessary information.

PART 2: WORKING WITH A TEAM

20 — Pass Your Knowledge Down to Others in Your Company

It's natural to try to one-up other people on subjects about which we have more knowledge. Some individuals freely pass their knowledge on to others and take the necessary amount of time to explain their thinking behind certain topics. Other people resist passing their knowledge on to others because they think that doing so might hurt them. Perhaps they think if they give their knowledge to other people then they will no longer be needed and may be replaced.

If you're living on borrowed time and don't learn new things daily, I can understand why you feel this way about transferring knowledge, because you may be passing along your entire knowledge base. The majority of people in the workplace are not desirous of passing their knowledge on to others in the firm. It is incumbent upon the upper management in the company to break people of this bad habit by training them to transfer their knowledge and rewarding them for this positive behavioral trait.

I used to work at a national accounting firm, and I was amazed at how some partners were unwilling to transfer knowledge to the junior employees in the firm. One day I went into a partner's office to ask him some questions about a job I was working on, and I was shocked by the responses that were provided to my questions. This partner was more interested in trying to confuse me than help me. I remember walking out of the office thinking, *I'm on my own in this company, and it's going to be solely up to me to make sure I learn the things I need to learn.* Fortunately, many other partners in the firm did not exhibit the same behavior.

CONSULTANT, CONSULT!

People who willingly pass knowledge down to others are secure with themselves and their ability to continue to learn and grow. They accumulate more and more knowledge every day. They have an uncanny ability to crystallize and boil down information and transfer it simplistically and effectively to others. They are natural leaders. They know that their efforts will create a better and more successful company.

Initially, the transfer of knowledge to an underling may be painful, but the senior employee knows at some point in the future this person will contribute and make their work life easier. The senior employee now has other people who can apply the knowledge to other jobs and issues, and this will free them up to learn more, create more, and further leverage their knowledge.

The employer will usually reward older employees for leveraging their knowledge by giving them promotions and great raises. If the company doesn't respond adequately to workers who are exhibiting these qualities, they will lose these talented people.

A model consulting company will fully leverage and exploit the knowledge of its key people in order to maximize the service being provided in the marketplace. If the key people are not passing the knowledge and experience down to their underlings, the business opportunity will not be fully executed. Ultimately, it's up to upper management to motivate their employees to push the knowledge down so that the firm can grow with a vengeance.

 How Do Teams Succeed?

Some service businesses create and produce their work product for the clients they serve by using a team approach. The team usually

PART 2: WORKING WITH A TEAM

consists of one or two team leaders who review the work, depending on the size of the team, and four to eight team members who prepare the work for the client's benefit.

The first thing a team leader needs to do is secure the trust and confidence of his team members. The team members need to firmly believe that the team leader has nothing but their best interests in mind and that he will do whatever is necessary to help them succeed and reach their full potentials. When problems arise, the team leader must stand behind his or her team members and fully support them as needed. Over time when a team leader consistently demonstrates this character, the team members will be grateful and will usually do whatever is necessary to reciprocate this trust and support for the team leader's benefit.

One thing a team leader should never do is degrade another team member in front of the client, as this will only serve to make the team a much weaker unit over the long term because the trust factor will be impaired. Another thing a team leader should never do is throw another team member under the bus as soon as a problem or conflict arises. The team leader must simply set clear expectations of what he or she wants the team member to achieve. The expectations should be job specific, individual specific, team specific, and always be in writing.

The team leader's objective is to attract and retain team members that can consistently meet the predetermined expectations. Team leaders should counsel members who fail to consistently meet the predetermined expectations. The team leader must realize that they are investing significant time in the team members. If a team member is not able to perform his or her job to the level of expectation, the team leader should take the appropriate steps to help the team member move on to a different opportunity—preferably sooner rather than later.

CONSULTANT, CONSULT!

The team should meet about once a week, in order to discuss the specific tasks that each team member plans to accomplish in the ensuing week. Some time should be set aside to talk about sticking points that need to be resolved. The meeting platform should be a two-way dialogue and all members should be expected to contribute to the conversation. The meetings should go at a rapid pace and no one should get too comfortable.

Team leaders should always be accessible and their door should always be open for their team members; however, in return the team members should be respectful of the team leader's time and use it wisely and efficiently. Team members should always try to take the initiative to make the team leader's life easier because the team leader has many more things to deal with in their day-to-day operation than the team member does.

A prudent team leader will place his or her team members in the areas where they can perform and excel best for the team. This requires the team leader to understand and properly size up the strengths and weaknesses of his or her team members. A prudent team leader will also put training in place for the perceived weaknesses of his or her team members so they can become stronger in their job overall and contribute more for the team.

When a team member does something well, the team leader should openly recognize the team member and give them credit where credit is due. Team leaders should give their team members full job responsibility, and when appropriate, the team member should be given a chance to present their work product to the client.

A team leader who holds the team member's hand, gives them little pieces of a job, and treats them like a baby is providing a huge disservice to the team member. In fact, team members have an obligation to themselves to communicate to the team leader

PART 2: WORKING WITH A TEAM

that they want more job responsibility than the team leader is currently providing under this circumstance.

Obviously, the faster the team member can demonstrate their ability to get the work done timely and adequately, the quicker the team leader will be to give responsibility. Ultimately, if the team leader does his or her job properly, the team members will emerge as team leaders as well and manage team members underneath them. A prudent company will place high value on team leaders who produce other team leaders because this by definition allows the company to grow.

22 — What Is a Team Leader Expected to Do?

Team leader is an important position within any company because an individual must be talented on many different fronts. For most companies, the team leader is equivalent to a partner. A team leader must lead and get results in many areas of the company's operations.

To do that, a team leader must develop mutual respect and bilateral trust. The team will be dysfunctional and not cohesive if mutual respect and trust are not initially established. The team leader should be looked upon as a role model for the other team members. The team leader must make sure the work product provided to the client is of high quality. The team leader has the responsibility to teach his or her team members in a manner that increases technical competency. The team leader must fully leverage his team members and monitor all team members to ensure they meet the job's budget expectations.

CONSULTANT, CONSULT!

The team leader's job is not to do the team's job. A prudent team leader will place heavy responsibility on his team members; most team members will appreciate the responsibility that has been given to them and will rise to the occasion. The team leader is expected to establish and manage client relationships to ensure that the company is providing the best service possible to the client. This requires the team leader to stay in constant contact with the clients through whatever means is necessary.

The team leader should also be viewed as a leader by his or her team members and should positively motivate team members to achieve their full potential. The team must believe the leader holds their personal interest in the highest regard. If a team leader does the job really well, they will produce new leaders. Team members should be a modified leadership clone of the team leader.

It is up to the team leader to establish excellent quality control and review procedures relative to the work product that gets provided to the client. They must use sound judgment when evaluating the level of review or quality control that should be applied to each unique situation encountered in preparing the work product.

A team leader is always instrumental in selling more work to existing clients so that the team can be fed. If taught properly by the team leader, the team members will also contribute to this effort as well. The team leader will really show their talent when the team develops new and different kinds of work product that are beneficial to the clients they serve. Broadening the bandwidth of client services above and beyond the typical services that the company provides is a powerful way of growing the company's business. This also allows the company to obtain new and different clients and may lead to other services that no one has previously considered.

The team leader is expected to act and think like a business owner and evaluate all things he or she does from this perspective. The team leader is also expected to think like an inventor that continually evolves and develops new ideas and refines old ones to be more efficient and effective in their implementation.

Obviously, some team leaders are better than other team leaders at executing the requirements described above; the company should go out of its way to be cognizant of these differences and compensate the superstar team leaders much more than the average team leaders.

Establish a Solid Review Process

There is a strong correlation between a company's internal review process of the work generated from within and the degree of its reputation in the industry in which it performs services. You will usually find that a company that has an excellent internal review process on the services it performs will have a solid industry reputation, and, of course, the opposite is true that a weak internal review process will usually result in the company having a lousy industry reputation.

If a services company has an employee preparing documents and sending them out to clients without someone else in the firm checking or reviewing the documents, then the company really has no internal review process in place. This exposes the company to the risk of having an inordinate amount of documents circulating in the public domain that may not properly represent the professionalism the company is trying to uphold. Odds are that there will be more mistakes on documents that lack proper review by others in the company.

CONSULTANT, CONSULT!

Obviously, there are lightweight matters of general correspondence from employees within the company that don't need to go through an internal review process; however, the company should establish a rule-of-thumb that requires its employees to seek an internal review of their work product when there are strategic or substantive items within the documentation being sent to the client. Strategic or substantive items usually refer to rendering advice, ideas, or opinions on the work product being transmitted. Rendering facts, your understanding of facts obtained from others, or general correspondence matters are not usually considered strategic or substantive. However, you must be absolutely confident that you have good facts when providing the client documentation that has not been internally reviewed by someone else in the company—*before* it's transmitted to the client. You should always caveat your understanding of the facts if you are not totally confident about the facts that you're providing to the client. You may further identify in the correspondence the areas that may need more research to sufficiently glean out the purported facts. This is a safe way to preserve your own professional reputation and the reputation of your employer.

A prudent services-based company will use anywhere from one to three levels of internal review of strategic or substantive documents prepared by its employees. If the documentation prepared by the employee is highly strategic or substantive, the company should use three levels of review. The first review should take place at the manager level, and the manager should spend an appropriate amount of time performing his or her review to ensure that the information is easy to understand and technically correct in every detail. The manager review is the most important review because the company allows the manager to spend whatever time is necessary to make sure the work product is accurate and correct.

The second review should take place at the partner level and the partner should spend an appropriate amount of time making sure

PART 2: WORKING WITH A TEAM

the facts support the conclusion reached in the analysis based on their years of experience. The partner's review is more top-level, usually focused on the executive version of the work product, and the partner should not be expected to math check and review every little detail in the analysis.

The third review should be conducted by a quality control person who is usually a different partner in the firm. The quality control partner has the broadest perspective of the company's work product that goes out to clients. Partners within the company may have varying ideas and opinions about certain topics and issues, and it's the quality control partner's job to meet with these partners and reconcile their differences so that the company has a consistent projection of its ideas or opinions to the clients it serves. As the company grows and more partners are admitted to the company, the quality control function becomes more and more important.

If the documentation prepared by the employee has little strategic or substantive information, then the company may only deploy one level of review by the manager. However, if the manager is unsure about the degree of strategy or substance that's being discussed in the documentation, then he or she should automatically seek a second review by the partner on the job. If the partner is unsure about the degree of strategy or substance being provided in the documentation and how it fits in with the firm's overall position, he or she should automatically seek a third review by the quality control partner.

It is extremely important that all personnel within the company fully understand their company's review process. Each person should know the role of the other people in the internal review process. For example, if the manager believes the partner will be math checking the documentation and the manager fails to perform this function, then the internal review process will have a hole in it and the possibility of greater mistakes in the work product will likely result.

CONSULTANT, CONSULT!

PART 3
IMPLEMENTING STRATEGY

CONSULTANT, CONSULT!

PART 3: IMPLEMENTING STRATEGY

24. Create an Intense But Low Stress Work Environment

There are as many different types of work environments as there are types of companies. Some environments are characterized by lackadaisical and unfocused employees. Other companies have work environments where employees are intense and stressed out in their day-to-day work efforts.

Common sense tells you that if the company's work environment is lackadaisical and unfocused, it is likely that the amount and rate of intellectual growth and development of the employees within such company will be low and slow. On the other hand, if the company's work environment is intense and action-packed, it is likely that the amount and rate of intellectual growth and development of the employees within the company will be high and fast. The latter instance is a preferred work environment for the employee who has big goals, but if too much stress is included in this environment then the employee may burn out.

A smart company will make sure management creates an intense and focused work environment, but it will also make sure that every effort is made to keep the levels of stress as low as possible. An intense work environment can be fun for everyone if management and the employees choose to make it fun. By making work that is action-packed and intense fun, the levels of stress of those involved will be lower. Management needs to coach employees to understand that the only expectation is that they do the best they can at whatever they are working on, no matter how intense or challenging it is. If you work hard truly doing the best you can at your work, and you end up with an unsuccessful result, you should still hold your head high and be proud of the intense effort that you put into the cause. In my younger years, when I was working at the national accounting firm, many employees worked very long hours (12 to 13 hours per day) in an intense but fun work environment. We kept it fun by telling jokes every once and awhile, going bowling, and playing softball. Laughing a lot is a great way to reduce stress.

Management should also train their employees not to take things so seriously, even in the midst of an intense work environment. Let the work be serious and let yourself be relaxed, because you will end up doing better work when you're relaxed than when you're uptight. If you have only an hour to prepare for a meeting or to meet a deadline, take a deep breath, go for it, and just do the best you can in the time allotted. Don't waste your time whining and complaining about the fairness of the situation; just focus and give it your best. You will be surprised by what you can achieve and how quickly you can achieve it when you remove the natural negative tendencies.

Most successful employees have trained themselves to ignore all the excuses that might normally arise when in this environment and put all their energy into buckling down and getting the job done. When working in a team environment, it is important that all team members work with these concepts in mind, because if one of the team members deviates from these concepts, it will cause distress to the other team members. Employees who work in an intense work environment with a group want to know that other team members are working together to avoid dysfunction.

PART 3: IMPLEMENTING STRATEGY

25 — Be a Fortune Teller

I have enjoyed watching my kids play soccer for several years and am still trying to figure out all the characteristics of a great soccer player. One characteristic, of course, is great anticipation skills. In other words, a great soccer player seems to know how to envision where the ball will be before it's actually there and be one step ahead of the opponent to capitalize on the play.

I am sure Abraham Lincoln anticipated and predicted that the Union would be held together because of the North's sizable population difference over the South, and the North's industrialization advantage over the South prior to the commencement of the Civil War. However, what he probably didn't anticipate or predict was the number of casualties that would take place on both sides to keep the Union intact.

In business, the vast majority of consultants go about their work with clients in a reactionary mode with little anticipation skills. If the consultant relies too heavily on the client for direction, however, the client may come to the conclusion that they should just do the task themselves.

An effective consultant is always one or two steps ahead of the process at hand. Another way of saying this is that the consultant is great at anticipating the process before it actually happens. Issues and tasks are identified, discussed, and evaluated in advance of the actual work being performed. Preparation gives the consultant time to thoroughly think through the issues and envision multiple solutions and outcomes.

CONSULTANT, CONSULT!

An effective consultant will take fortune telling to a higher level of excellence when they have a high degree of accuracy in advising the client as to what is going to happen and it ends up happening exactly in the manner predicted. I enjoy telling a client exactly how a meeting will play out in advance, then going to the meeting and watching it occur as predicted.

After the meeting, it's rewarding to see the excitement in the client's eyes about how well we prepared and predicted the issues and concerns that arose in the meeting. Clients love consultants who have an uncanny ability to tell them exactly how the meeting will transpire and end.

Of course, the only way the consultant garners their visionary fortune telling capabilities is through years of experience and preparation—and from learning from the best.

Harvard professor Tom Lehrer said it well: "Think as you work, for in the final analysis, your worth to your company comes not only in solving problems, but anticipating them." Not sure what to anticipate? Talk things over with your supervisor. Leverage his or her experience. Then "wow" your clients.

26. Always Identify Client Opportunities

Some people are naturally skilled at identifying opportunities. Most opportunistic individuals are positive in personality and a have tremendous amount of ambition and determination. It's almost like their brains never stop processing ideas and opportunities to pursue. Even in the most unexpected situations, an opportunistic person seems to find the diamond in the rough.

PART 3: IMPLEMENTING STRATEGY

The opportunistic person is just not content until they find good ideas to put into action. Unfortunately, being opportunistic requires the exertion of a lot of daily energy and some people are unwilling to extend themselves to the degree of exertion that's required to be effective. Additionally, a successful opportunistic person requires a continuous string of ideas over an extended period of time versus one-shot or one-time only events. In the consulting business, it is imperative that the consultant comprise such characteristics. Some consultants innately embody this characteristic and others must force themselves to obtain it through experience and practice.

The process of identifying client opportunities in the consulting business is analogous to being creative, inquisitive, and results-oriented. It's not enough to simply perform a consulting job in a perfunctory or mechanical manner. An effective consultant will identify other client-related opportunities from the work at hand. For example, when engaged in performing a specific set of tasks, the opportunistic consultant will identify additional ideas or advice for the client to consider. These opportunities or ideas should revolve around adding value that would generate income for the client, maintain or reduce costs, maintain or reduce business risk, or get the task done in a timely manner.

The consultant's lifespan with the client will be greatly increased if this opportunistic approach to consulting is deployed. A client relationship should be viewed as a continuum and not a one-time event. If the consultant processes their job in a robotic manner without bringing client opportunities to the table, then they will find their client relationship to be more like short-term employment.

Clients appreciate the consultant who adds value and who identifies opportunities. Most clients will view a consultant in a cost-benefit way. A client would be remiss if they failed to realize the benefits

CONSULTANT, CONSULT!

of using a consultant who provides services that are a net financial benefit to their bottom line.

There are some clients, of course, who do not do a good job of distinguishing the tangible benefits of a consultant who identifies job-related opportunities. In this case, the consultant should explain tangible benefits that accrue to the client as a result of their efforts in identifying client opportunities.

I had a meeting one time with a national homebuilder client of ours to discuss our company's billing invoices. We had worked with this particular client for many years and, quite frankly, I felt like the client representative was getting awfully petty with his questions. After listening to more and more pettiness, I began to get somewhat frustrated.

I said to the client representative, "We have billed you about one million dollars over the past several years and increased your profit by 30 million dollars, so why aren't you using our firm more if we're getting you a 30-to-1 payback ratio?"

The client responded by asking for documentation to support my 30 million dollar profit claim. I proceeded to specifically account for the details off the top of my head at the meeting—making it very clear and easy to understand.

At the conclusion of the meeting, the client representative agreed to pay the outstanding invoice issues, primarily because I described the tangible benefit derived from our services.

Whenever possible, help your clients see the value of working with you to seize the opportunities before them.

PART 3: IMPLEMENTING STRATEGY

27. Always Know Where You're Going— No Joyriding

Since the consulting business is an intellectual business, it is essential that your mental characteristics be clear, concise, and organized. Many people in the workplace fail to understand why they are doing what they are doing. They meander and dabble along without a conscious idea of what they are trying to achieve. If you ask them what they are doing, they answer in a vague and general way.

You must force yourself to know—in advance—the specific purpose of your work. Not knowing your purpose is like driving to an unfamiliar destination without any directions. How can you expect to reach your destination? You might get lucky and find your destination after missing it a couple of times. However, this is no way to conduct your business affairs! Your client is paying your bill, and they most certainly aren't interested in paying for joyrides.

I remember a young, entry-level staff accountant at the national accounting firm I formerly worked for. He was asked to prepare a very simple tax return for a client. In fact, it was so simple that about 10 numbers needed to be filled in on the tax return forms. When the billing invoices came out a couple weeks later, I saw the partner in charge running down to the young staffer's office to complain about the 200 hours he spent preparing this simple tax return. The young staff accountant just didn't know where he was going and failed to ask for help along the way. Ironically, this young staffer made some adjustments to his work approach and ultimately became a very good consultant.

In the consulting business, or any other business for that matter, a 30-day rolling to do list is a useful tool for consultants who have voluminous tasks that need to be performed and prioritized on a daily basis. This list should identify the project and the specific tasks that need to be performed with the responsible person assigned to the task. A ranking format can also be used to help prioritize which tasks should be done first.

You must clearly and specifically write out the task so that the task's purpose is clear to all parties. Another useful tool is to develop a listing of all the steps necessary to complete the job. This list will help the consultant see the big picture—and then act upon it.

Chris Corrigan, co-owner of Richard Branson's Virgin Blue, couldn't agree more enthusiastically. "You can't overestimate the need to plan and prepare," he says. What's more, "You really can't over-prepare in business."

28 Know Fact from Fiction

Have you ever met a person with a tendency to exaggerate, inflate, or blow things out of proportion? Do you find yourself mentally dividing what they say by a factor of two or three to get to the real story?

Sometimes the information we get from supposedly reliable sources is blurry. I get nauseated when listening to the news or reading the paper because these institutions often seem concerned with giving their own institutional spin instead of stating the facts of the situation. Thank goodness for the Internet because we can now go research information that we're interested in and dig as deep as we want to in order to get current facts about a particular situation.

PART 3: IMPLEMENTING STRATEGY

In business, one of the quickest ways of losing credibility is to make statements or form conclusions that are inaccurate. Implicit in the consultant/client relationship is the sense that the consultant provides truthful information, without exaggerating. It comes down to a matter of trust. Does your client know, deep down, that he or she can trust you?

If I'm around someone who appears to be loose with facts, I feel like I have an obligation to make them and others more factually accountable to the conversation at hand. I may do this by asking for their source of information or asking whether they reviewed another pertinent source of information. Obviously, if the source is good then chances are what they are saying may be accurate (unless they didn't spend the time to properly digest the information).

Consultants must work hard to make sure they have performed enough research to know if the source of information they are relying on is accurate, because this information is the foundation on which their ideas and opinions are based. One method of obtaining good facts is to know the best sources of information for the topic. If you don't know, then you should talk to someone who does know. You should always ask yourself, *What is it that leads me to believe this is the most factual information available on this topic?*

After securing the facts about a topic or situation, you must interpret the information and formulate statements or opinions from these facts. If you're not careful, good facts can be twisted, leading to fictional consulting and the risk of losing your credibility. Good fact-finding is where you get the ultimate power in the consulting business. Your opinion on a topic is interesting for conversational purposes, but in order to get real horsepower behind opinion, factual information must be included. This approach will always set you apart from the rest of the group.

CONSULTANT, CONSULT!

I had a meeting with one of my clients who was selling their property to another land developer. The other land developer brought along their own consultant to represent them on certain financial matters that were the topic of the meeting. This consultant was making statements or issues based on purported facts of the property that would cause the property value to be reduced, thereby benefiting his client.

Once the consultant was done pontificating his issues based on supposed facts, I proceeded to pull out excellent source documents that proved his supposed facts were incorrect, which then led to his statements or issues being incorrect. The client was extremely disappointed with his consultant representative, who ended up being discredited.

The very next day, I received a call from the consultant's client, who asked me if I could work with him on some of his other projects, as well as the project we discussed the day before. Knowing fact from fiction was the key to success in this case. This new client knew he could trust me.

29 – Think Like an Entrepreneur, Not a Professor

Most individuals in the consulting business have a college degree. Our educational system at the college level in the United States is excellent. Proof of this is the fact that all kinds of people around the world attend our colleges. College professors inspire students and provide a foundation to take into the working world. However, college professors tend to have large egos. It seems like the colleges that have good reputations often have professors with the biggest egos. A student should be cognizant of this and avoid adopting

PART 3: IMPLEMENTING STRATEGY

this character trait, because large egos don't do well in the business world.

Many college professors have little experience in the world outside of academia. This is undoubtedly a problem because if the teacher is disconnected from the working world, he or she likely will not be able to provide his or her students with meaningful examples of how the course content relates to the world of work. Some professors may be teaching theory and practice on a topic that simply is outdated and no longer applicable.

A prudent student should ask, *How does what I'm learning work in business?* Things that students can do to help themselves find the answer to this question might consist of joining campus clubs that are connected to businesses, securing an internship, and most importantly, trying to identify someone they may know in the business community with whom they can establish a mentoring relationship. A student who does these things will get much more out of their education, as well as gaining a jump-start on understanding how to think more like an entrepreneur.

Successful consulting businesses have employees who act more like entrepreneurs than college professors. Entrepreneurs don't have time for egos. They know how to get things done swiftly and efficiently, and they know real-world work experience is what makes them great in performing their job. They know that college experience gave them basic tools but taught them little about how to understand and thrive in the business world.

I remember working on a real estate transaction with a consultant who was a Ph.D. and a college professor, representing a municipality. My client, a homebuilder, provided this consultant with specific information about actual home sales that were occurring in the residential subdivision. The professor consultant made adjustments to the actual home sale information, however, under the assumption that he had a better understanding of the marketplace—because, after all, he was a college professor.

This consultant simply let his ego get in the way of business, and he was rather embarrassed when he was called on the carpet to prove that his adjustments to the sales prices were more appropriate than the actual real-world home prices that homebuyers were closing escrows on. He just simply could not prove it because reality is reality.

Always Surround Your Consulting Services Around These Things

Many companies lack vision—both in *what* they are doing and *where* they are going. These companies usually start with a good service or product, giving them the ability to establish a viable business, but they fail to adapt to changing circumstances. Sometimes these companies fail to understand the needs of their clients or customers. They also may not understand how their company's service or product is being used by clients or customers.

A smart company will understand how the client or customer is using their service or product. A company also must understand its competition and strive to outperform the competition by differentiating its services and products. If true employee passion is developed behind the service or product being provided, this can be a way of creating differentiation. For this reason, successful companies never stop trying to understand how to develop employee passion in the workplace.

PART 3: IMPLEMENTING STRATEGY

In the consulting business, every service or product provided should be centered on how to raise the client's income, assist in reducing or controlling the client's costs, or reduce/control the client's risk. In doing this, the consulting company itself has a significant opportunity to thrive and grow.

A consulting business that performs value-added consulting for its client's bottom line will undoubtedly retain clients and get more and more work from those clients. The realization percentage of accounts receivable collections will also be significantly higher when using this approach to business.

So, ask yourself:

1. What's your company's vision?
2. What are you doing?
3. Where are you going?
4. What are your strengths?
5. How good are your products or services?
6. What do you need to do to adapt to changing circumstances?
7. Would your clients or customers agree?
8. How are they using your products or services?
9. Are they tempted to use your competitors' products or services instead? If so, why?
10. In what ways is your company striving to outperform the competition?
11. Have your employees become passionate? How could you further cultivate such passion?
12. When it comes to the bottom line financially, how are you helping your clients or customers?

CONSULTANT, CONSULT!

31 Don't Play the Consulting Chaos Game Like Others

Some individuals enjoy chaotic environments, but most do not. Most people like to have a straightforward conversation where, after the conversation has ended, they have a complete understanding of what was discussed. Nothing is worse than having a discussion with someone and ending up more confused than you were before the conversation started!

Some people are poor communicators and are willing to admit it; others remain in denial. Some people like to create confusion around certain topics because of ulterior motives lurking behind their actions. They may be smart like a fox trying to manipulate something to their advantage, or they may not know what they are really doing, and they put up a smoke screen to hide deficiencies.

In the business setting, you need to make note of the people you are dealing with who appear to be creating chaos in the job you are working on. You need to determine the motive behind their actions. Some consultants purposefully attempt to make situations seem more complex than they really are. Perhaps they are doing this to justify their employment with the client. Maybe these confusing consultants want the client to believe the job is complex in order to establish job security, charge the client more, or spend more time on the job. Some high-priced consultants and attorneys play the consulting chaos game with their client to justify their large hourly billing rates.

A prudent consultant must put an end to the consulting chaos game as soon as he or she can for the benefit of the client. The client doesn't know what you know, so it is incumbent upon you

PART 3: IMPLEMENTING STRATEGY

to educate the client about the people involved in the job who are playing on confusion for their personal gain. After all, the client is paying the bill for the people involved in the job.

An experienced consultant will challenge the others on the job who are creating the confusion by forcing them to explain concerns, and the consultant should respond to each concern by boiling it down to simplicity. Each excuse or point of confusion must be challenged directly with all decision-makers at the table. This process will allow the client to begin to see the clouds of confusion clear up and a straightforward understanding of the topics or issues discussed will become evident. A great consultant knows how to break down confusion and complexity and make it simple and easy to understand.

The fox-like consultants or attorneys who are playing the consulting chaos game are always the hardest ones to flush out. They might have close relationships with some of the key decision-makers associated with the job. The smart consultant's technical competency alone may not be enough to stop the madness, and you may be required to resort to politics as an additional means of achieving your goal.

Ultimately, your client will appreciate your insightfulness and concern about making sure the job is being processed in a straightforward manner.

 You've Got to Get Organized

We all have difficulty keeping things organized sometimes. It seems like the more time goes on, the more we accumulate, and the

CONSULTANT, CONSULT!

harder it becomes to keep things organized. People who are naturally organized have a recurring process of moving new things in and old things out. Others wait until things are completely piled up to reorganize themselves. Procrastination and organization are oxymoronic. You simply must organize yourself on a regular basis and not wait until the end of a task.

In my mind there are two types of organized people: those who organize for the sake of organizing but are unable to find what they are looking for when they need it, and those who organize in a manner that makes them efficient and effective at what they do with the information they have organized. The latter takes sufficient time up front to think through how they should organize information and the purpose for organizing it in the first place. This advanced planning allows them to know exactly where they can find the information. People who are organized are typically mentally organized, whereas people who are not organized are usually mentally disorganized.

I have worked with many people in business, and it's interesting to note that if a person's filing system or method of organization is good, they're usually fairly well organized in everything else they do in their job. Everyone will suffer on a job that does not have an organized foundation. I don't want to overemphasize the importance of good organization, because there are people who are very organized but spend way too much time organizing their files and documents.

One time I reviewed a young consultant's work product. As I was going through the documents, I asked him to provide me the supporting documents that he drew certain financial conclusions from. Every time I asked to see his supporting documents, he would go back to his office and scour through drawers but claimed he could not find the documents. At one point, he was outside looking in the trunk of his car for the documents.

PART 3: IMPLEMENTING STRATEGY

Needless to say, this consultant was having difficulty organizing his work product.

Ultimately, I couldn't take much more time with this consultant because of his disorganization, so I called upon his manager to assist me in finishing my review. The manager was also having difficulty showing me source documents and became very frustrated. Ironically, all the source documents that needed to be reviewed were sitting in the files I was reviewing. The young consultant was simply unorganized and the manager was simply frustrated because the source documents were not exactly in the sequence that he envisioned. Each had organizational problems, just different kinds.

The key to good organization is to organize in the shortest amount time necessary so that you can quickly access the information when called upon, as well as understand its content. Good organization of files will help develop a mental construct to remember what the documents say. The use of an index and tabs are helpful. One tab could be for all general job correspondence. Another tab could be to separately identify an important document. Microsoft® OneNote and EverNote are useful software programs. Electronic organization should be done in the same way, and all jobs should have duplicate physical and electronic files in the unfortunate event that the electronic files become corrupted.

What Are You Doing to Grow the Company?

Many employees don't consider their jobs beyond the paycheck. They only do what is required in performing their daily work routine. As soon as the clock hits the standard workday time, they head for the door and don't think one minute about their job until they arrive the next day. Some employees selfishly focus on individual needs and fail to ever think about the needs of the company they work for. Of course, there are some companies that operate in the same selfish manner.

Prudent employees will not only think about their own needs, but they will attempt to understand the company's needs because they understand that the employee and the company are mere reflections of each other. Wise employees figure out how to conduct their work efforts in a manner that will benefit the company. In doing this, both the employee and the company will grow and prosper.

The automotive industry in the United States is a good example of what can happen to a company when its employees become most concerned about their own needs and fail to understand the connection between themselves and the company. Everyone at General Motors, for instance, should wake up and realize that the only way this company will survive is to be the premier leader in manufacturing cars that run on alternative energy sources. This would allow General Motors to continue to grow and pay its United States labor force the high wages they are accustomed to. If the employees don't get involved to make this happen, they will see their jobs go overseas to a labor force that requires significantly lower labor costs.

A smart employee will provide ideas to their company's management and owners that can help the company grow and flourish. This employee will invest his or her time to develop new ideas, products, and services that will contribute to the company's growth. Management and owners will undoubtedly appreciate this person's efforts and listen attentively to what he or she has to say. Good companies with strong leaders at the top should go out of their way to support an employee who exhibits this type of behavior.

This constant interaction between all the employees working as a big team will grow the company by definition, and, in turn,

PART 3: IMPLEMENTING STRATEGY

new economic opportunities within the company will become available. Companies can grow in both good and bad economic times—you just have to work much harder in bad economic times to achieve growth.

A company will always hold in the highest regard the employee who gets work-related results first before asking for anything. Financial success doesn't lead anything. It simply follows those who create good ideas that result in company growth.

34. Of Course Those Are Good Ideas, But Which Is the Best?

It seems there's never a shortage of ideas. For any given project or topic, some ideas will be highly appropriate and others can be unrealistic and too farfetched. The real trick is to figure out which idea is the best because we all have limited time, energy, and resources. Careful thought must be put into analyzing which ideas are the best so that time is not wasted on the implementation of all of the ideas.

People who are always providing ideas about a topic are usually characterized as creative and have a tendency to view things from many different vantage points and perspectives. A prudent person will listen attentively to another person's idea and act as a sounding board in an effort to further develop the possible merits of each idea.

Too many companies take the shotgun approach to deploying their ideas by expanding their workforce in many different directions with no real targeted, strategic plan. In consulting, however, toss out the notion that the more ideas you throw at the client the better the chance that something will stick with them. You should be careful and considerate of your client's time and only present the best ideas to them. Bombarding them with too many ideas will only create the negative appearance of over-selling yourself.

You and your company must determine which idea is the most appropriate and most cost-beneficial for your client, given your client's business environment. The idea could have great cost benefit results for the client, but if the client is not conducting enough business in the area to which the idea relates, the lack of business volume would render the idea not appropriate at this given point in time. When the business volume picks up in the relevant area, it may then be appropriate to revisit the idea and present it to the client. The company should also understand the client's competition, or lack thereof, when weeding through ideas.

An idea that is a logical extension of a company's existing services is always a good place to start when attempting to select the best ideas for a company to capitalize on. The company already has a built-in audience of existing clients for whom they are performing services and to whom they can present their new ideas. For example, if the company assisted a client in establishing a special-purpose entity that will last for several years, they could also help in the ongoing administrative requirements of such entity. The company can easily get meetings with existing clients to present your ideas. If the idea is cost-beneficial, the existing clients will likely engage your client's company to perform the additional related service.

As a consultant, you should also evaluate a company's core competencies when sorting through ideas. For example, if the idea is an income tax-based idea and the company is not in the business of providing tax services, you will probably choose not to capitalize on the opportunity because there are plenty of tax attorneys

PART 3: IMPLEMENTING STRATEGY

and tax accountants who also specialize in doing this type of work and have better qualifications to do so.

An idea that fills a true need in the marketplace is an excellent idea to capitalize on. Ideas that fill an important niche in the marketplace usually bode well for companies providing these services. However, if the barrier to enter is low and the idea is commodity-based, the competition will likely jump on this idea shortly after its deployment. If the barrier to entry is steep and the idea is not commodity-based, your client's company will have an excellent opportunity to fully exploit the idea, and you should move forward immediately.

Clearly Understand the Risk/Reward Model

Risk is everywhere and in everything we do. Even the little things we do—like driving to work—carry risk. It's impossible to eliminate risk in our lives no matter how hard we try. What's more important than trying to spend time eliminating risk from our lives is to understand risk, recognize the different degrees of risk, and manage risk accordingly. It is sometimes difficult to recognize the degree of risk in what you're doing because we live in such a complex society with a multitude of laws and regulations. If a person has little or no understanding of the laws and regulations that apply to what they are doing, they will not be able to properly identify the risk they may encounter.

In the services business, the risk/reward model refers to the notion that money you receive for the service provided is commensurate with the degree of risk the company is assuming relative to the possibility of being sued if you make a serious mistake in the service provided. For example, it would make no sense for a company to provide a service that renders little pay, and in return, carries a high degree of risk. A company that operates this type of risk/reward model will usually have difficulty surviving over long periods of time.

There are situations, however, where a company may consciously choose to operate this type of risk/reward model under limited circumstances. The company I work for performs disclosure work for our clients, and this disclosure work is high-risk work because mistakes could lead to litigation. Our company has decided to consciously perform this service because we are the most qualified company to perform such work, and we are the primary leader in doing the work or transaction that relates to the disclosure work being provided. Yet, the best position for a company to be in is to provide services that render significant pay and carry a low degree of risk.

There are many different methods to measure the degree of risk you may be assuming when preparing work product for your clients. Before you start an engagement with a client, you should always ask the client how they plan to use the work product. For example, if a client plans to use the work product to submit to a lender or potential investor, you should recognize that this is a high risk job. Furthermore, you should establish a budget that is sufficient to perform the work necessary given the level of risk and plan on a comprehensive internal review by others in the company.

On the other hand, if the client plans to use the work product for internal use only, you should recognize that the risk profile is low and the budget and internal review process should be adjusted accordingly. It is important to note that you should always attach a cover letter to the work product that is being provided to the client that recites the work performed and its intended use in accordance with the representations made by the client. This helps protect you and your company in the event that a client says one thing and attempts to do another with the work product.

I remember preparing a cash flow feasibility analysis for a real estate client which was supposed to be for internal use only, and our cover letter stated the same. A month or two later, I found the cash flow analysis included in the sales package of a national real estate brokerage firm that was soliciting the property for sale across the United States. Our cover letter was not included in their package, just the cash flow analysis. Obviously, if a lawsuit were ever to occur, we could produce evidence that the work product was never to be used for this purpose.

Another method of measuring risk relative to the work product is to understand how the client and other third parties have historically used the work product that you are being asked to prepare. You may think a work product carries high risk, but the historical precedence may indicate that in practice it carries low risk. Part of this evaluation should include talking with others in the industry and determining the degree of lawsuits filed relative to the work product.

Each employee in the company should take the appropriate amount of time before engaging with a client to fully understand the risk associated with the work product they are providing.

Everything Is Negotiable to a Point

Yes, it's true; everything is potentially negotiable! Some people spend their whole lives negotiating every little thing they run across. It almost becomes a game for them. I believe you should spend time negotiating the important things and not waste time negotiating the little things, because it's usually not cost beneficial.

Furthermore, people get a little tired of interacting with someone who is always negotiating every little detail. The consummate negotiator implicitly believes he or she will always be better off negotiating every little detail, but he or she fails to understand the old adage "penny wise, pound foolish."

I think it's important to know when to negotiate and when not to negotiate. Don't negotiate for the sake of negotiating because your negotiating power and effectiveness will probably not be as good as it could be if you were more selective in your approach.

The bottom line to negotiating is to negotiate with common sense and good logic. Honesty is one of the best personal characteristics necessary to be a successful negotiator. If the opposing side considers you dishonest or not trustworthy, you will have a difficult time succeeding in your negotiation. Most successful negotiations usually result in both sides believing they got the best result possible with the understanding that each side did not get everything they wanted.

Traditional sit down face-to-face negotiations are always a good thing to do, but I think egos can get in the way of the negotiation, especially if there are a large number of attendees. Oftentimes, consultants and attorneys feel like they're under the spotlight and have to go out of their way to show their own client that they're adding value and properly representing them. There is nothing wrong with this type of representation as long as the consultants and attorneys don't end up being deal killers due to their small ears and big egos.

One of the keys to being a good negotiator is to fully understand the goals and objectives of each side that's negotiating, and to craft a plan that works for all of those involved. A prudent negotiator

PART 3: IMPLEMENTING STRATEGY

will always attempt to find the hot buttons of the parties involved in a negotiation. A good plan for negotiation is to negotiate on the hot button issues and provide ideas that result in exchanges between these hot button items that capture the intrigue of the parties negotiating.

Sometimes it's helpful to assign monetary values to the hot button items so the parties can have a better understanding of the value of what they may be exchanging and/or receiving. Of course, if the opposing side has assigned a higher value to a hot button item than my side's calculation of value, I may use this information to my advantage even though it's not surprising that different people will have a different idea of what something is worth.

I personally like to negotiate before the actual negotiation date, if possible. Oftentimes, I am in a position to be able to talk to the opposing side's consultant or attorney about some of the deal points that are being considered in the negotiation. I usually negotiate with the understanding that I have no negotiating authority, and this tends to bring the defensive walls down with the opposing side's consultant or attorney. The consultant or attorney will provide a similar response regarding their authority to negotiate.

This "no authority" to negotiate ironically creates the best platform for negotiating. This setting gives me ample time to talk openly and frankly with the consultant or the attorney, and usually what happens is the consultant or attorney will have follow-up conversations with their client and I will do the same with my client to obtain relevant feedback.

Significant progress can be achieved through this side negotiation process. This process may take several iterations back and forth to get close to making a deal or perhaps even securing a deal. If the side negotiation process is done properly, by the time the actual face-to-face meeting occurs both sides will simply state their positions that have already been discussed ahead of time and everyone can shake hands and formally make a deal.

37 Set Short-, Mid-, and Long-Term Professional Goals

As each New Year approaches, I am anxious to hear the personal and professional goals of my friends and family. New Year's Eve is one of the pinnacle points in the year during which people pause to establish their goals for the forthcoming year. Unfortunately, for most people, within a few months little action has actually taken place. Many people even forget their goals!

A strong test of your character is measured by how well you set goals and how well you actually achieve the goals. It's akin to "walking the talk and not just talking the talk." Goal-setting can be painful because you are willing to place personal accountability on yourself. At the end of the day, you have no one else but yourself to blame if you fail to achieve your goals. For most people, the safest route on this matter is to simply not set any goals at all or to set easily attainable goals so that they don't set themselves up for possible failure.

In business, all employees should set short-, mid-, and long-term goals for themselves. The short-term goal spectrum usually ranges from daily to weekly, the mid-term goal spectrum usually ranges from one to five years, and the long-term goal spectrum is usually beyond five years. Implicit in this three-tiered approach to goal-setting is linkage, in that, if the short-term goals are achieved as projected, the person will then be in a position to achieve the mid-term goals, and if the mid-term goals are achieved as projected, the

PART 3: IMPLEMENTING STRATEGY

person will then be in a position to achieve the long-term goals.

Initially sit down and write out specific goals that you want to achieve over these three timeframes. After initially establishing your goals, you should revisit them on a regular basis. The short-term goals should be viewed daily because these goals are most susceptible to change and modification when new situations necessitate adjustment to the goals. It's fine to be flexible with your short-term goals and modify them as necessary, as long as such goals still fit logically into your mid- and long-term goals.

When you take the initiative to establish written goals, you should share your list with your employer and other company cohorts in order to obtain feedback and refinement. This feedback is important because some of the goals may be unrealistic and inconsistent with the business plan of the company. For example, you may want to develop a new service line for the company you work for, but the employer may want you to focus more energy at expanding an existing service line because the cost benefit of doing this is more appropriate given the circumstances. A prudent employer, however, should be extremely open-minded and less critical of your goals because you may be seeing an opportunity that your employer just doesn't see. And it could be a really big opportunity.

The employer must keep in the back of their mind that an employee who unconditionally establishes goals by his or her own initiative probably has tremendous passion and interest in accomplishing those goals.

By sharing your list of goals with your employer, he or she will also be in a better position to assist you in achieving those goals. An employee who takes the initiative of setting professional goals, without being told to do so, is clearly a self-starter and a leader.

CONSULTANT, CONSULT!

An employee who is given goals to achieve from his or her employer is a non-self starter and a follower.

The ultimate measure of goal-setting is the actual achievement of the goals that were set. This is where many people fall short and find all kinds of reasons why they did not achieve their goals. This is where the personal accountability factor comes into play. You must force yourself to objectively evaluate how well you performed in achieving your goals.

The more objective and honest you are with yourself about your successes and failures, the better you will become at learning how to achieve the goals you set. An employee who is highly effective at achieving his or her goals will always be personally and monetarily enriched by his or her employer.

38 — Understand the Forest Before You Look at the Trees

We all seem to get stuck from time to time in the daily routine: completing the work our job requires, going home at the end of the day, and doing it all again. Routine can cause us to stop paying attention to what is going on around us and how the world is changing. We bury our heads in work detail and stare at tree trunks.

Today the world of business is changing and information travels at an incredibly rapid pace. Sometimes opportunities are right before your eyes, but you fail to see them because you are myopically focused and immersed in the daily routine. You have to take time to understand how your company, your job, and your work fit in with the big picture.

PART 3: IMPLEMENTING STRATEGY

One time I was working with a manager who was my supervisor on a job. Many people in the firm I worked for considered him to be really smart because of his educational background. As the job progressed, I noticed he was extremely detailed on the nuts and bolts of the job. I initially thought, *this is great and I stand to learn a lot from this engagement.* However, as the days went on, I realized that he really had no idea how his detailed job applications folded up into the bigger job picture. As the years went by, he never changed in his job approach and eventually left the consulting business. I guess he was just not wired to see the forests and the trees.

Employees should track and disseminate data that is relevant to the company so that it can adjust with the changing times. This data should be shared with others within the company so everyone is aware of changes. An insightful company will forge ahead, understanding mega trends in times of changing industry.

Before an employee buries his or her head in work detail, they should understand how their work fits into the economic backdrop. The process involved in understanding the big picture usually starts with grasping a sense of what is going on globally. Global trends in business are usually the hardest to understand.

Trends in the U.S. economy are important to review in order to understand how your company might be impacted by its changes. For example, are interest rates going up or down? Is the national economy accelerating or slowing? What new technologies might change the way the company performs its services or produces its goods?

The next level of analysis is to understand how the industry you work in will be impacted by national economic trends and local market trends. Have you done your homework yet? If so, what are the top five trends that will affect your clients? See what's coming before your clients do. Then make sure they know how to seize the opportunities (and avoid the threats) that lie ahead.

CONSULTANT, CONSULT!

What Are the Attributes of Selling Work?

Compiling the right attributes when selling work to prospective clients will give you the competitive edge needed to walk away from a meeting with more work. The first step is to meet with the right person at the prospective client company. Every company's employees perform many company functions. You may find yourself meeting with an individual who isn't the appropriate person to be talking to about the services you're trying to sell. In these cases, figure out the prospective client's point person and later place a phone call to schedule a meeting with the correct employee. Then you can find out if your company will be able to meet this company's needs.

Without sounding presumptuous or appearing unprofessional, find the balance between explaining the services being offered and the resulting financial benefits to the clients bottom-line. Once you discover a way to meet the client's needs, demonstrate knowledge about the services being offered. The likelihood of success will increase significantly if you are aware of what sets your company's services apart from the competition. Obviously, the more experience you have relating to the services being discussed, the more likely you'll succeed in gaining the client's business.

As previously mentioned, come prepared to client meetings with a list of references. Always have fresh ideas to apply to the prospective client's project so they get an idea of your strategic thinking abilities and competency. Additionally, be prepared to explain to the prospective client why they should hire you or your company. Exclusive client representation is a great example of providing

PART 3: IMPLEMENTING STRATEGY

differentiation since many consulting companies work with diverse clients.

If you were unable to sell your or your company's vision at the meeting, follow up with the prospective client until they tell you they have decided to use another company. You must be consistent and persistent so the client clearly knows you want their business.

The more you learn about a company's history, current realities, key players, and future direction, the better you'll be able to sell your consulting services. Become an expert on your prospective clients. Know more than some of its own people, but be careful to drop one fact here, another there, casually. Don't tip your hand. Instead, let them figure out you're serious about winning their trust and helping them reach their future goals and objectives.

When you talk about other clients of yours, be specific about the results you achieved, but only hint at those clients' identities. After all, you want to keep the focus on how you can achieve similar results for your prospective client. The more enthusiasm you have over how your consulting firm has helped other clients, the more likely new clients will retain your services.

40 Quickly Understand Your Company's Business Philosophy

When a new hire joins a company, that individual only has a general understanding of the company's philosophy, vision, and service to clients. Everything about the company is new. Given this reality, the new employee should chart a plan to understand as much as possible about the company. This might include getting to know

CONSULTANT, CONSULT!

other employees, which provides a broader understanding of what each individual does within the company, along with identifying the personalities, strengths, and weaknesses of the individual employees. If you have hired a new employee, encourage him or her to utilize your company's resources. This might include reading through materials and manuals, attending seminars, and utilizing video/audio content posted on your company's intranet. Encourage them not to feel guilty about "not doing anything productive." Learning is job one for any consultant.

If you're a new employee, ask questions relevant to all current tasks and projects. Initially, write down all such questions. Then look for answers the company already has documented internally. Write down important answers you want to learn by heart or know how to find quickly. Then start interviewing other colleagues and senior management to answer any remaining questions.

Remember, the first 60 to 90 days of employment are used to assess your aptitude, skills, and abilities. Your role as an employee is to embrace the company's vision and become an effective member of a team, so do excellent work. In return, you'll receive compensation and recognition, typically by management. Such accolades might then afford you the opportunity to advance, become a partner, and begin a successful career.

At every stage in your career, keep learning about your company's business philosophy. "It's what you learn after you know it all," says John Wooden, Hall of Fame basketball coach, "that counts."

PART 3: IMPLEMENTING STRATEGY

41

Focus on Your Offense and Minimize Your Defense

I worked with an attorney on a real estate transaction for a mutual client. This lawyer's basic background was in litigation primarily and secondarily in transactions. As we met to negotiate with the opposing side, I noticed the lawyer's comments were mostly defensive type comments. It was a rather awkward situation for me because my business approach and style is quite different.

Every time I attempted to move things forward in an offensive manner, I found our lawyer moving us backward with his defensive type comments. It felt like advancing six yards but being penalized five yards, so our real net gain amounted to one yard. This transaction ended up taking a lot more time and costing the client a lot more money because of the defensive natured lawyer on our team. If you share that lawyer's tendencies, minimize them quickly!

Many offensive strategies can be deployed to attain business results. Take the initiative to schedule client meetings, and come to the table with a prepared agenda. Before closing, set a date for the next meeting and assign tasks to members of the team that must be accomplished prior to reconvening.

If team members come to the next meeting and fail to deliver the information you were anticipating, take the initiative to politely but professionally reprimand them for their lack of preparedness. Set the stage for expectations to be reached.

A good offensive strategy in business implies that the employee initiates proactive measures that, in turn, require a response. We all tend to get bogged down with work and what needs to be done. However, an offensive strategy will elicit employees who are seeking to meet client needs proactively.

Don't forget the sage wisdom of famed football coach Vince Lombardi: "The difference between a successful person and others is not a lack of strength, not a lack of knowledge, but a lack of will."

Think of yourself as a quarterback. You will undoubtedly take control of things and influence the process of productivity your way. Most people avoid the offensive posture in business because it's harder to do and more risky than simply taking a defensive posture. Yet it's those on the offense who will strategize and achieve success!

42

Cut Your Losses Sooner than Later

An investment should yield results. Nothing is worse than investing time in something only to discover that it was a fruitless expenditure of effort. Most productive individuals realize this and strive to minimize waste and maximize net benefit.

In order to be successful in business, you have to establish parameters that determine when to cut your losses. Such parameters should be set to minimize the time needed to make such a decision. It might be painful at first, but in the long run, cutting losses earlier will save time, resources, and frustration for all parties involved.

If you're working with new clients who are disrespectful or unwilling to pay their bill for services, it is probably prudent to cut your losses. Remember, there are too many great clients to work for in

PART 3: IMPLEMENTING STRATEGY

the world; time is too short to be interacting with a client who doesn't want to conduct business in a professional manner.

You also may need to cut your losses if you have an employee who is underperforming. Management spends significant amounts of time training employees and a manager typically discusses such concerns with a management team. Within a few months of working with an employee, the manager should be able to determine if the employee is a good fit for the company. If the employee is not a good fit, the manager should cut the company's losses by letting the employee go.

In my early years of growing the business, I learned this the hard way. There were a handful of employees that I gave multiple opportunities to succeed, only to find that for whatever reason they were just not interested in jumping on any firm opportunities. I presented them with opportunity after opportunity and nothing seemed to stick. I spent many sleepless nights trying to determine the talents these employees had so I could develop ideas for them to get excited about. I presented them with different opportunities because their job performance had been historically substandard. After giving them three different opportunities over several months, I realized that they just didn't care. I felt like I was the only one who really cared about what the firm was trying to do for them.

Today, I am still willing to try these tactics, but I can assure you it will not be over several months. Instead, it will be over a much shorter timeframe. In the end, it's better for the company and for the ill-fitted employees, as well.

The old business adage is still true: "Cut your losses and let your profits run."

CONSULTANT, CONSULT!

43 — How Do You Beat the Competition?

Competition is engrained in the free market system of the U.S. economy. Some industries face steeper competition than others. Highly competitive industries have low barriers to entry. Some companies have managed to establish business models that have large barriers to entry relative to competition.

For example, some consulting companies will require professionals to be knowledgeable and technical about many disciplines (such as law, finance, politics, and engineering). How well the consulting company and its employees master these disciplines will determine the steepness of the barrier to entry relative to the competition. Therefore, one way to beat the competition is to establish a business model that minimizes competition by producing goods or services that have large barriers to entry.

Another way to beat the competition is to know everything about your competition. Since the company is usually only as good as its employees, you should profile key players to best understand individual strengths and weaknesses. Strategy is the key to understanding the competition and utilizing ways for your company to retain success.

Of course, marketplace realities change over time. Periodically evaluate your company's products and services. Are they still in demand? Are there still high barriers to entry?
As well, periodically evaluate your competitors' products and services and key players. What do you need to add, drop, or change to keep a distinct competitive advantage?

PART 3: IMPLEMENTING STRATEGY

Never use the excuse that you're not at the top of your game because of all the competition out there. "I have been up against tough competition all my life," Walt Disney said. "I wouldn't know how to get along without it."

Don't bemoan the competition. Instead, do all you can to compete against them and come out on top again and again.

Avoid the Sheep Herd

Many companies cluster employees in large groups with varying levels of compensation depending on experience. Government agencies are a prime example of this. One employee may be in group 5 and another may be in group 10 because of their tenure and experience. The employee will often get pushed up the compensation ladder by virtue of just staying with the same employer over time and not necessarily because of their performance. Most motivated employees become frustrated with this means of compensation because it does not benefit individuals who excel faster than others.

If possible, work for a company that avoids the sheep mentality when compensating employees. Otherwise, you and your colleagues may become frustrated by the lack of opportunities and benefits. Ultimately, the result can be a mediocre team approach toward work or the loss of good employees. I personally experienced this in a national CPA firm that I used to work for. I was instrumental in establishing a new service area, which contributed significantly to the growth of this company. I developed the ideas, sold the ideas, and worked with a small team to execute the ideas relative to the new service area. I also worked late nights and most weekends to develop this work to its fullest potential.

— 95 —

CONSULTANT, CONSULT!

In the office next to mine was a peer who was given work to do by the company. This peer simply did the work given to him and worked mostly the hours from eight to five. At the end of the year when raises and bonuses were given, I received about the same raise and bonus as my peer did because the company was more interested in keeping everyone in the sheep herd rather than individually rewarding them for the merits of what they achieved for the company. I was simply amazed at how a company could fail to see the difference in what I was doing for the company versus what the peer was doing for the company. I was a market-maker and the peer was an order-taker. The firm was simply not structured to compensate a market-maker differently than an order-taker, and after experiencing several years of frustration, hoping they would change their ways, I decided to move on and start my own company.

If you work for a company that encourages strong teamwork and rewards individual performance, great! Do all you can to be properly rewarded year after year.

Also, remember that rewards come in different forms. Beyond raises and cash bonuses, take into account the value of all of your employee benefits. And consider asking for added non-cash bonuses if you're excelling at your job. Non-cash incentives can include bonus vacation days. Just be sure to request these a year in advance if you reach certain measurable goals. Of course, be very discreet at every turn.

Again, look for a place where you can work hard, be successful, and be compensated accordingly. Then cultivate loyalty, do your best, and enjoy the rewards that come your way. Why settle for less?

PART 4
WORKING SMART

CONSULTANT, CONSULT!

PART 4: WORKING SMART

45 — One Time Right: No Badminton Please!

For most individuals, procrastination is a way of life. The more they procrastinate the better they get at it. We start more and more things, but as time moves forward these things fall by the wayside and rarely do we finish a fraction of what we started. Some consultants believe they have greater job security if they never finish their work or if they extend the work over a protracted timeframe. Don't do this! A successful consultant will finish what was started and find ways to complete jobs in the most effective, business savvy way possible.

The organizational structure of a typical consulting firm functions like a pyramid with the partner, manager, and associate involved in preparing client work. The associate typically spends the majority of time on the engagement. The manager usually spends about one-fifth of the time that the associate spends reviewing and providing detailed comments on the work product. The associate then revises the work product as needed based on the manager's comments until the manager is satisfied. Sometimes, a vicious game of badminton can occur between the associate and the manager wherein the work product can get passed back and forth with little improvement to the product.

This inability to get the work done on time or in the first sitting increases the client's cost. The associate should take time to thoroughly review his or her own work so that it can be reviewed by the manager. The associate needs to research relevant issues prior to submitting work product to the manager for review. The expectation of completing the review process in one sitting between the partner and the manager increases when the aforementioned steps are taken.

I stumbled upon the heading to this chapter based on one particular experience I had with some co-workers. I was the partner on a job working with a manager and an entry-level associate. I would stop by the manager's office periodically to determine when I would receive the work product so I could review it. He responded by saying he was in the process of reviewing the work and I would have it in a couple of days. After those days went by, I again stopped by the manager's office to ask him the same question as before.

Well, needless to say, after stopping by three different times and getting the same response each time, I decided to sit down in the manager's office and look at the work product files to see where the job was at. There were over 15 pages of manager comments directed to the associate—on 10 different dates spanning over three weeks. There was little redundancy in the manager comments, thus each comment sheet was essentially a new set of comments for the associate to respond to.

This was one of the most vicious paper-passing badminton games I had ever seen. I explained my concerns about passing work papers back and forth so many times and the inefficiencies that occur. The manager agreed; he hadn't realized how much back and forth activity he was doing with the associate. I also emphasized the importance of trying to give the associate all of his comments at one time, if possible, instead of 10 different times.

PART 4: WORKING SMART

46
Know What You Know and Know What You Don't

The world is full of people who seem to always let on that they know a lot more about a subject than they really do. How many times have you had a conversation with someone who purports to know something about a particular subject and after a minute or two you find that they really don't know anything about it?

In the consulting business, clients expect consultants to have all the answers to their questions, so by definition there is significant pressure on consultants to perform. The client expects this because the consultant usually carries a high price tag. Their assumption is that you should have all of the answers to their questions or problems.

If you fail to meet the client's expectations, it is possible that the client will seek another company's expertise. Though you might be lacking specific experiences or knowledge relating to the client's questions, it is appropriate to provide a preliminary opinion about a topic. However, guard against caveats and follow up with the client at another time if research on the topic is necessary.

It is acceptable to tell your client that you either don't have an answer to their question or need to do a little research and get back to them with an answer. These strategies give you credibility and help your client understand that you want to provide accurate information even if you might be able to come up with an answer on the fly. Providing your clients with accurate information gives you credibility and solidifies your professional reputation.

Demonstrating to the client that you are always careful to provide them with an accurate answer to a question they may have shows them that you have genuine care and concern about making sure you are providing them a high degree of certainty that your answer is accurate. The consultant should always pause and take their time to thoroughly think through the answer to a client's question. It's always helpful to think out loud with the client so that the client can fully appreciate the mental analysis that you are going through to evaluate the answer to their question.

From the client's perspective, they need a consultant who is highly accurate in his or her advice, because the client will often make economic decisions based on the advice given. Clients are always looking to hire the consultant who has the best reputation of being highly accurate in the advice they give. The prudent consultant will always convey a very high percentage of accurate information to a client because they know the client will come back to them again and again for advice, and they will also refer other clients to the consultant because of the success they have achieved from the consultant's advice.

Henry T. Ford was a dynamic person who accomplished many things, with one of his most notable accomplishments being the establishment of the Ford Motor Company in 1903. Beyond being dynamic, Henry seemed to have a good grasp on knowing what he knew and knowing what he didn't because he usually surrounded himself with highly capable people. He once quipped, "Anyone who stops learning is old, whether at twenty or eighty. Anyone who keeps learning is young. The greatest thing in life is to keep your mind young."

So, don't be a know-it-all. Keep learning. Your clients will respect you all the more if you do.

PART 4: WORKING SMART

— 47 —
Operate in a Continuous Questioning Mode

When I was 18, I toured a drywall manufacturing plant. While on the tour, one young man touring with me asked question after question about the plant and its operations. He would write down his questions on a pad of paper along with the answers. He was a lightning rod full of energy and intensity. I had never met anyone so eager to learn and absorb information.

As I listened to his stream of questions, I realized the power of this guy's approach to learning and saw firsthand how he was setting himself apart from the rest of the students. The simple fact was that he was fully engaged in learning as much as possible about everything. I'm sure if I found him today, he would be running a company. This guy impacted my life, and almost immediately I began to adopt his approach of asking questions to facilitate the learning process.

Sometimes people who are always asking questions can get on your nerves. No doubt there are certain times and places where asking lots of questions can either be appropriate or inappropriate. In business, however, it is acceptable to ask many questions. There are very few circumstances where this could or should be perceived as a negative. You will notice that the person who asks lots of questions is usually a top performer in their company. Not surprisingly, they often have a higher IQ. Of course, this assumes the questions are reasonable. Those who ask too many silly or obvious questions are typically not listened to or taken seriously by others.

My rule of thumb is to ask a minimum of 100 questions while working on any particular job. Obviously, 100 isn't a magic number, but it reminds me to remain investigative and ask as many

— 103 —

questions as appropriate for me to do my job in the best and most efficient way. Asking meaningful questions is a learned process so the only way to improve is to start using lots of question marks. Technology now allows us to compile a database of questions and might prove to be an effective way for you to manage information you gather. If you don't organize your questions and answers, of course, you will not remember them. If that happens, you may find yourself caught in a circular mode, asking the same questions over and over. Avoid that trap at all costs.

The sooner you adopt a continuous questioning mode approach in business, the sooner your business picture will become clearer. Again, your goal is to understand and then apply your knowledge, insight, and wisdom. Don't jump to conclusions before you truly grasp the issues before you.

As you compile your database of questions, begin with the six core questions every investigator or journalist or consultant asks:
    Who?
    What?
    When?
    Why?
    Where?
    How?

From these six core questions, you'll quickly compile dozens of specific, relevant questions for the job at hand.

PART 4: WORKING SMART

48

So You Can't Work Without a Computer

Computers don't do the work. Yet as a culture we've become increasingly reliant upon them to get anything done. The computer is nothing more than a tool of assistance. A computer screen is simply a blank piece of paper and the keyboard is a pencil.

One day at work, one of the younger associates in the firm where I work came in and told me that she needed to work from home the next business day. She further told me that she would not be able to get any work done because she would not be able to get to a computer.

As I heard this, it dawned on me that so many young students coming out of college are too dependent on the computer. I wondered if this person ever stopped to think about how people got their work done before the personal computer was deployed in the business world.

So many people spend an inordinate amount of time staring into the computer screen when at work. It's almost like they believe all the answers to their work-related problems can be solved by gazing into the computer screen.

The fact is a computer and all the wonderful applications that exist within a computer can distract you from doing the things you really should be doing in your job—if you're not using it properly. For some people, the computer is an entertainment device for them to gaze at while at work as they toggle nonchalantly between email, instant messaging, and the Internet. Because of the newness of all the latest computer applications, it's easy to get caught up and distracted from the things you really should be focused on when working.

CONSULTANT, CONSULT!

In the consulting business, you should use your computer applications sparingly and focus your energy on getting thoughts clear in your mind, reading documents printed on paper, and preparing outlines of documents or spreadsheets prior to working on the computer.

One of the biggest mistakes I have seen with consultants is that they don't spend enough time thinking through their format and approach to a word or spreadsheet application before jumping onto a computer terminal. Good planning will always provide greater efficiency, and this will ultimately save your client money.

The human mind is the most wonderful computer of all, and as a successful consultant you will want to spend plenty of time processing information and ideas before sitting down and working on a computer. Your mind runs the show—not the computer! I personally wonder how much the computer and the Internet have contributed to the ups and downs in our global and national marketplace since the year 2000. Many companies have built sophisticated software programs that assist them in making decisions—whether to do or not to do something, or to buy or sell something based on the input variables. Many of these programs have been insufficient in the real world, and, unfortunately, many companies have gone out of business because of this. Who would have predicted the fallout in Wall Street firms in 2008 alone? Even Alan Greenspan admitted that many of the Federal Reserve's economic models did not contemplate some of the economic fallout that occurred in the credit and financial crises that commenced in July 2007.

If you're searching the Internet for information, force yourself to stay focused on the task at hand. Far too often it is easy to get lost amidst the sheer volume of information—simply a mouse click away. So if you are using the Internet to do research, then stay disciplined; search only for the information you need and avoid distractions.

PART 4: WORKING SMART

In the end, a consultant doesn't sit at a compu' sults. Make sure you do too!

Say It in 10 Meaningful Words or Less

Most of us obtain information on a daily basis from a variety of sources. Most of our inboxes are overflowing, readily testifying to this fact. The increase in information presents a dilemma. How do we digest this information, retain the necessary components, and apply it to our busy lives?

First, learn how to disregard meaningless, inconsequential data. In the consulting business, you need to be respectful of your client's time. Assume that the time you have with them is limited, unless they indicate otherwise. Since your client contact airtime is limited, come prepared to ask questions or make comments on issues in the most efficient and effective manner possible. Whenever possible, attempt to ask questions or comment in 10 words or less. Learning how to boil down technical business information and convey it in 10 words or less is something you can learn to do through a number of years of practical work experience. The more you practice this, the better you get at it. It never hurts to practice this boiling-down approach to communication in your personal life as well. However, don't get caught up in expecting your friends or relatives to do the same because most people have a tendency to ramble on when they communicate in a personal setting.

A consultant who fails to learn how to communicate concise information in 10 words or less runs the risk of losing the client's attention. Monitor your client's attention span and adjust the scope of conversation accordingly. After meeting with a client, evaluate

CONSULTANT, CONSULT!

your communication skills. Were you succinct? Did you meet the client's needs adequately? How can you improve?

I had a meeting with another consultant to obtain some project information in order to finish a job. I had about 10 questions to ask this person. After the first question or two, I noticed that he was taking an extremely long time answering each question. As I sat, listened, and took notes, I noticed how little of substance was on my notepad. I also found myself having difficulty paying attention because he just simply talked too much.

Without running the risk of being rude, I tried to increase my level of participation in the conversation in the spirit of getting some answers to my questions. I wanted to move on with getting my job done! The consultant still continued to ramble on—almost like he was reading a story from a very thick book. I tried the best I could to get to the bottom line of his responses, but it was a real struggle. It's safe to say this person did not subscribe to "saying it in 10 meaningful words or less."

One word of caution on this matter is that you should avoid the trap of watering down the bottom line approach in a manner that conveys an inaccurate picture of what you are trying to get across. This should be avoided at all cost, and it may mean that more explanation is needed in order to accurately convey the information. This should take precedence over watered downed punch lines that run the risk of conveying an inaccurate statement.

Remember, clients appreciate consultants with the uncanny ability of recognizing the bottom line, efficiently communicating the plan/vision, and providing a concise and accurate picture for review. If you failed to get the point across, then you failed to effectively communicate!

Bottom line: Be concise!

PART 4: WORKING SMART

50

Memory Is a Must

Going through school, I placed little regard or importance on mental memory. I considered memory to be the lowest level of the thinking process. After spending years in the consulting business, however, I garnered newfound respect for the importance of memory.

A consultant lacking mental memory or the ability to recall important details relating to the client's work will probably be unable to provide that client with wise advice. After your initial work, you should be able to answer all relevant and factual questions relating to the project. Review those details regularly to keep your memory sharp. Give priority to any details you can't readily recall at a moment's notice.

If a person is unable to answer such fundamental questions off the top of their head, and instead has to refer back to the files to provide such answers, it is likely this person does not have a good memory. It is possible that the person is simply not very interested in what they are doing. If this is the case, you probably have a different problem at hand.

Management within the consulting company should set expectations up front with their staff: that they are required to have an excellent memory relative to the important details on the job. An excellent memory helps establish excellent facts that the consultant and others can use to provide excellent analysis for their clients.

Another test of memory skills is to bring a consultant to a client meeting. After the meeting, the consultant's supervisor should converse with the consultant and evaluate how well he or she was able to retain information discussed. Did he or she remember the important details or simply superfluous details?

If you struggle with certain memory skills, purchase a self-help book and begin working on improving your recall. It is also helpful to work on your listening skills as there is a direct correlation between listening and memory skills. Your goal should be to do more than hear words. Instead, actively listen. Your posture and other body language will impress clients. Why? Because they know you're fully engaged as they answer your questions.

As you assimilate new information, meet with a colleague following your client meeting to review all of the pertinent information you just learned. Then write it all down as soon as possible. Otherwise, that new information will fade like a Polaroid® picture in reverse. Write everything down—or lose it.

Beyond writing it down, study what you've learned and commit it to memory. Then start using it. What we repeat we actively remember far longer than facts duly noted and left unattended.

Never forget: Memory is a must!

51 Get Done Now, Not Later

It is human nature to put things off, and we're all guilty of falling into this habit. However, it always takes extra energy to get a project done later. In part, it can be difficult to mentally recall something that occurred days ago rather than something that occurred earlier the same day. By doing something now, you'll save yourself a lot of time and energy in the long run.

PART 4: WORKING SMART

Also, minimize the number of times you pick up something and put it down. Every time you pick it up again means starting over again. Avoid such repetitive wasteful motions and inefficient thought processes. Instead, prioritize the things you are working on and try to get things done sooner rather than later, even if the deadline is days away.

Also, the smaller items that are less important can be delegated to others if you are in a position of being able to do this, or you can complete them later. Either way, you will be much more productive overall.

In the consulting business, clients usually want something *now*. You might find yourself becoming frustrated because you are handling multiple jobs and clients quite frankly don't care about the jobs that are unrelated to their job. Therefore, it's important for you to ask the client some basic questions to accurately measure their needs from a timing perspective. Just because a client *wants* something done now does not necessarily mean they *need* it now. Once you've agreed to a delivery date, fulfill your professional duties and responsibilities to the client to the best of your abilities. Work hard and fast. Whenever possible, beat your deadlines. But don't overpromise. It's much better to ask for more time upfront, even if you know it might be possible to finish the task(s) sooner.

In the real estate consulting business that I work in, our client's top priority is to keep their projects on track so timing is extremely important to them. They have so many tasks that cannot be completed until other tasks are first completed. Sometimes, to a fault, the client is so focused on meeting dates and deadlines that they end up sacrificing the quality or financial opportunity that may be present in a transaction.

The consultant should always avoid the pitfall of getting a client's job done on time at the expense of poor workmanship or quality or lost financial opportunities. I realize that sometimes you just have to get done with the job because that is the client's desire, but if the quality is not to the consultant's and firm's professional standards, then the consultant must properly disclose this to the client in writing to preserve his or her professional reputation. A quick email to the client expressing your concern that more research or investigation should occur on a particular topic, which could result in a different conclusion in the final analysis, is an example of an appropriate disclosure. However, try not to make a habit of this, and always try to avoid at all costs being put into this situation. Always remember the consultant's professionalism needs to be considered sacred and held in the highest regard.

Among other things, carefully add holidays and vacation days into your schedule up to a year in advance. That way, you won't be surprised when a particular month has fewer work days than average.

Also, add occasional "catch up" days on your calendar. Do all you can to keep those days appointment-free. You'll be amazed how productive and refreshed you feel each time.

Always remember: Successful people get things done—now, not later.

52
When Your Attitude or Patience Gets Thin, Get More Sleep or Take a Vacation

The typical busy life has resulted in most of us over-extending and over-committing on a regular basis. Such obligations can be exhausting, resulting in working too much, resting too little, and not providing the best possible service to one's clients. When this

PART 4: WORKING SMART

occurs, one of the best remedies might be a vacation. If you're not careful, however, vacations can be stressful and overwhelming too. So it might be helpful instead to utilize resources found at a health club (such as yoga) to clear your mind and improve your attitude. Do whatever is needed to keep your mind and body focused and energized.

As a consultant, it is imperative that you're able to maintain a good attitude when with clients. Therefore, it is important for a company to have mechanisms in place to help identify members of the team that might be exhibiting problematic behaviors or attitudes. Some employees may feel as if they were treated unfairly by the company, others may be struggling personally, and still others might be overwhelmed by life. Whatever the reason, it is important for the company to meet with the consultant, discuss the behaviors or attitudes witnessed, and attempt to remedy the situation.

I remember working on a job with a manger in my younger years. We were all working very long hours at the time, but this manager was over the top on hours. He might as well have brought in a cot in order to sleep at the office. He was working about 16 hours a day, six to seven days a week, on a big project that was going on for several months. The problem was that his attitude and patience were wearing thin as each day went by. His yelling increased and ultimately he began to throw things—sometimes at other cohorts. He was simply feeling too much pressure and was most certainly well into the burnout phase. Upper management finally came in and forced this manager to take a small vacation and cut back his work hours.

Your company will thrive only when you're working with a healthy team. It might be appropriate to suggest that some employees take a vacation or a few days off work. Whatever the solution, the sooner something is done, the better the results will be long-term for all members of the team. When each team member is a healthy and balanced individual, then the team will be healthy too.

Does your team have a big project coming up? You might consider encouraging specific team members to take a couple of vacation days before starting that project. Afterward, reward the most productive team members with a couple of bonus vacation days. Your team will be happier and more productive for the long-haul. Be sure to take care of yourself, as well.

Where's Your "To Do" List?

Creating a "to do" list is essential in the business world. In fact, you might have more than one to do list. I think it is human nature to resist using one because most people truly believe they can keep it all in their heads. However, the fact is that you will forget certain things, or you will fail to do them in a timely manner if you don't write them down somewhere.

Those resistant to the idea of using a "to do" list are consciously or unconsciously admitting that they don't want to be held accountable. Personal productivity and your ability to get things done will increase significantly if you incorporate the list into your daily routine. So make a list, then track and monitor your progress.

To do lists are especially helpful in managing deadlines and other time-sensitive matters. A well orchestrated and implemented to do list will not only elevate your professionalism, it will enable you to be more efficient and effective. You'll deliver much better results for your clients or customers on a regular basis.

PART 4: WORKING SMART

Use your to do list to break down large projects into a series of smaller assignments. You'll find it easier to get started and repeatedly feel rewarded by all the progress you're making.

Be sure to prioritize your list. Remember, priorities can be subjective, so regularly revise your to do list. You may want to add several quick time-sensitive steps to the top of your list at the beginning of each day. Those easy victories will jump-start your productivity and generate positive momentum that will carry you through the remainder of each day. The list should be viewed several times a day and modified based on the new information that comes your way each day. The list should be clear and concise, and the tasks should be written with the fewest words possible that precisely describe what you or someone else needs to do. Since this document is viewed several times a day, the person should be able to quickly gaze through it.

If the list becomes too cumbersome, the person may run the risk of not using it enough because they may feel it requires too much administrative effort on their behalf. You must continually force yourself to keep the list simple and clear because it can get cumbersome and weigh you down. This must be avoided at all costs or you will end up no longer using it.

Another common pitfall is that a person writes a task on their to do list that is too conceptual or simply summarizes the status of a job. A good test to determine if your tasks are clear is to have someone else review the task and determine if they can clearly ascertain the specifics of what needs to be done. If they cannot read it and go execute it, then the task is not clear enough.

Increase your personal productivity and everyone wins—you, your company, and your clients.

Know what to do—and do it!

CONSULTANT, CONSULT!

54 — Monitor Your Stress Level

Consulting is a high stress field and, if you're not careful, it can lead to burnout. Your days are probably filled with deadlines requiring constant reprioritization. You start off your day thinking you will be accomplishing certain things only to find out that everything has been changed. You go to a meeting thinking you will be talking to one person and when you walk in the room is full of 20 people who want you to give them a seminar on a particular topic. Of course, you were not prepared for this, so your stress naturally increases.

As you continue to grow as a consultant, to do lists will increase along with your other job responsibilities. There are times where you may fall into the trap of preparing work product by yourself because you know you can get it done quicker and more efficiently than delegating tasks to your staff. In your mind, you may think you're the only one in the company that can do what you're doing, or no one else can do it as well as you can. If that's true in your case, you're on the path to burnout. Turn around—quickly! Otherwise, once you burn out, you'll have to set a course for personal recovery and then get your career back on track.

A few steps you might want to consider if you're at risk for burnout.

1. Quit trying to control everything. It's a huge contributor to burnout. Instead, resign as manager of the universe. Keep reminding yourself that micro-managing hurts everyone—including your clients.

PART 4: WORKING SMART

2. Seek help from members of your team and learn to delegate. Learn to enjoy teamwork. Share in the responsibilities—and rewards.

3. Don't develop unrealistic expectations for yourself. Ask for more time. Leave room in your schedule to breathe. Add more "catch up" days and vacation time in your schedule.

4. Dismiss the idea that you're indispensable. Your company was smart enough to hire good employees. Prove it by teaching them what you've learned. Don't forget that experience is the best teacher—especially learning from other people's experiences.

5. Take a team member to client meetings. Give them the opportunity to run the meeting with the understanding that you're there for support and backup if needed. Applaud their ability to gain more experience, skills, and confidence under your tutelage.

6. Cultivate a grace-filled environment. After all, perfection isn't a perfect way to live. True, most things have to be done right the first time, but allow room for mistakes. Instead of losing your cool, maintain a good sense of humor. What feels like a disaster today will be a good story someday.

7. Balance life's demands. You're a human being, not a machine. Avoid too many extracurricular activities that will drain your energy. But life is more than work. Have at least one or two positive, healthy pursuits outside of work. You'll enjoy life more and be a more productive, less stressed person on the job.

CONSULTANT, CONSULT!

55
You Can't Be Shy or Insecure in This Business

Everyone has unique personality traits, but in the consulting business, not all personality traits are beneficial. For instance, shyness and insecurity are something we all experience at times, but a successful consultant cannot afford to exhibit such characteristics. Even when life circumstances leave you feeling insecure, it is of utmost importance that you still appear confident in client meetings. If you're unable to perform at full capacity in a client meeting, it might be best to allow another team member to serve in your place until you're able to return with confidence.

You simply cannot be shy in the consulting business. You must force yourself to break out of your shell. You may want to enroll in a public speaking course or attend a motivational seminar. Oftentimes, shyness can be overcome with passion. By building a positive support system within the company, individuals who are shy will be granted the opportunity to achieve. And in turn, the company should reward them with encouraging feedback.

If an individual is either unable or unwilling to combat shyness, then they might be better suited for a less demanding company position. Because the bottom line is that a successful consultant is one with a secure sense of confidence.

If your feelings of shyness or insecurity are getting in your way, examine whether any of these three common fears may be the root cause.

1. *The fear of rejection.* If you worry about what your boss thinks, meet with him or her. Without naming your fear, let them know

your need for occasional words of affirmation. Explain that you find it easier to be productive when you know your boss is happy. Once you know they are happy, don't worry about what your client *might* be thinking about you. Instead, dismiss the fear of rejection out of hand.

2. *The fear of failure.* Typically, a consultant has to work harder to fail than to succeed. True, mistakes can be made, but to truly fail is tough work indeed. You're smarter than that if you're reading this far. Besides, you have a good team around you. Ask questions to draw on their decades of experience and success. Remember the old adage, "It's better to try and fail than not try at all."

3. *The fear of success.* Yes, some individuals fear doing exceptionally well. Usually, it's because they want to avoid the limelight and pressure of performing at that high level month in and month out. Avoid such "all or nothing" thinking. Instead, remember that key victories can provide welcome momentum and respect for months or even years to come.

Establish Low, Mid, and High Mental Gears When Working for Clients

When it comes to processing written information, there are fast readers and slow readers. Many people believe that fast readers are smarter than slow readers. Though this might sometimes be true, we should never infer that a quick reading speed equals a more effective means of capturing a solid understanding of the content.

CONSULTANT, CONSULT!

Some speed-reading schools advertise that you can learn to read a book within an hour with a high level of comprehension. I think these schools send the wrong message and fail to understand that effectiveness is much more important than efficiency.

A person can appear to be highly efficient at what they are doing, but at the same time never effectively achieve tangible results. They may run around the office with tremendous confidence and energy, and they may be great at communicating with clients, but they may have little ability to sit down and focus on the client's needs.

A prudent consultant must be both efficient and effective in performing work for their clients, and must know how to properly balance these two factors. Balancing these factors is like a stick shift in a car that has low, medium, and high gears. The consultant is smart enough to realize there are times were the mental low gear needs to be applied because of the complexity of the material. A good example of this would be writing or reviewing legal documentation, when the consultant must slow down and carefully read each word one at a time. I call this "peck-reading" because one must focus slowly and carefully on each word. In such cases, speed is simply not that important.

In other situations, the consultant should use their mid mental gear to process the information they are working on. This mid mental gear is appropriate when the consultant is fairly familiar with the information he or she is working on and has spent significant time in the past researching data and information germane to the work at hand. The work itself would be considered average in terms of its complexity.

The consultant should use their high mental gear when very familiar with the content of the work. This work is characterized as procedural or non-technical in nature. A good example of this would be processing administrative memos, client emails, and client voicemails.

PART 4: WORKING SMART

The prudent consultant will not operate at one given speed for all mental endeavors at hand. Instead, different mental speeds will be applied based on the nature of the work he or she is doing in order to achieve both efficient and effective results.

Be proactive in making a written list of how fast you want to work on specific tasks. Your format can be very straightforward, as shown below. The results will speak for themselves.

Low Gear (emphasis on effectiveness)
1.
2.
3.
4.
5.

Mid Gear (balanced emphasis)
1.
2.
3.
4.
5.

High Gear (emphasis on efficiency)
1.
2.
3.
4.
5.

CONSULTANT, CONSULT!

57
These Things Will Get You Fired

Certain basic standards of conduct must be employed in your daily work efforts—both with co-workers and with clients. When an employee falls below these basic standards, the company has an obligation to discipline the employee for these actions. Not only is this important for the sake of the offending employee, but it is essential for his or her well-behaving co-workers. If the company fails to take appropriate action in a timely manner, the action could be perceived by others as acceptable within the organization. The company must rid itself of employees who exhibit cancerous behavior.

Unfortunately, there may be times when you have an employee who is dishonest or a chronic liar. Employees that comprise these characteristics are dangerous to the company, their co-workers, and the company's clients, because you can never get a straight answer from a chronic liar. They're too busy trying to cover up their past lies and determine how to weave in new lies. You simply cannot get factual or accurate information from chronic liars. It's difficult to determine a person's degree of honesty through the interview process. References are the best way to check on the person's integrity, but this is no guarantee either. If you discover your employee is a chronic or habitual liar, let them go as soon as possible.

An employee with a bad attitude is another kiss of death of which the company must rid itself. Workers within a company already have enough stress in their day-to-day affairs, and they don't need the added dose of bad attitude from someone else in the company. A bad attitude creates a negative work environment, and this negativity wears on other employees over time. Some employees may latch onto

PART 4: WORKING SMART

another person's bad attitude and this negativity can spread around the company like cancer. Most people will naturally stay away from a person with a bad attitude, but you don't always have that luxury. Raising your voice and yelling at others in your company is another attribute that is completely unacceptable. You don't need to yell to get your point across, no matter how frustrated you may be with an individual. A good employer will set clear and direct expectations about what someone else is to do on a team project. The person either meets or doesn't meet those expectations, and yelling at them isn't going to give them any added means of meeting those expectations. If you feel as though you are coming close to yelling at someone, simply take an immediate break from that person and take a walk to clear your mind. Remind yourself that yelling doesn't work—it's simply overrated and outdated. Yelling can often be a tactic used by management to minimize the interaction that the manager should be having with his or her staff. Clearly, the staff person isn't going to be interested in going into his or her manager's office if they get yelled at each time.

Not showing up to work on time is another area that will result in termination if it falls outside the normal range of attendance. Tardiness shows a lack of commitment or interest in the job, and if the employer doesn't crack down on these actions it can spread to others like a bad infection. One employee I knew was always tardy for work because, without his company's knowledge, he was also working a side job. The company was unknowingly paying for this person's efforts related to his side job until he got caught.

Depending on the actions of the employee and the degree of such actions, the employer will need to either immediately terminate the employee or give them one warning with termination to follow on the second offense. It's important to note that no one in the organization is exempt from the enforcement against these actions, including the owners of the company.

CONSULTANT, CONSULT!

58 — Are You Being Reasonably Productive?

Productivity means to produce something, to create, and to be efficient at what you are doing. Companies use all kinds of different tools to measure the productivity of their workforce. A company manufacturing a product can fairly easily measure the performance of its employees. Measurements such as the cost per product or the labor hours per product are easily understood and can be compared over time to measure productivity.

Unfortunately, in the service industry it's more difficult to measure productivity because the product is produced intellectually. Measuring intellect is difficult because it is so esoteric. How do you measure how fast one person can produce, create, or be efficient at something compared to another person when the human mind is at work to accomplish these tasks? Companies in the service business use standards such as billable hours, or a comparison of actual billable hours to budgeted hours to measure productivity, but these tools still fall short of capturing real productivity.

A company in the service business will probably have more success in achieving productivity from their workforce by identifying the things employees do in their day-to-day work that makes them unproductive. Simply eliminating these unproductive habits will by definition increase the employee's productivity.

There are a multitude of wonderful tools that have been provided to the services sector over the past decade that help employees become much more productive. However, these tools and software can also be used improperly in the job environment and serve to actually be a net loss to the company in terms of productivity.

PART 4: WORKING SMART

Surfing the Internet for personal things while at work is a habit that is unproductive to the company. This can become an addictive habit that can get completely out of control. The employee's use of work email for personal purposes also hurts the employee's productivity. The use of instant or text messaging for personal purposes is extremely distracting and lowers the person's productivity. Talking on the phone for personal purposes while at work doesn't help matters either. As wonderful as these tools are for productivity and communication, they can also serve as big distractions. Most companies realize they need to develop ways of monitoring their employees in these activities in order to establish a means of measuring productivity.

Eliminating all the distractions in your daily work is the key to becoming highly productive. Productive employees don't spend time conducting personal business on company time. In the business of billing hours for services, the client will ultimately become the beneficiary of the employee's productivity because their bill will be lower.

I remember checking on an employee who had worked on a job with me. The employee was supposed to be preparing a specific document for a client and significant time had already been charged to the job. I asked the employee to show me the specific document so that I could see the progress. The employee returned to my office about an hour later to show me the documentation, and unfortunately it was clear that he had taken a document from a similar job and simply changed the client name, but he failed to realize that the document he provided was completely unrelated to the job at hand. I realized the hours he charged to the job were fictitious and he was terminated for his conduct.

A prudent employee will be reasonably productive at work and respect the notion that the company and the company's client have the right to expect them to be productive. From the time you start your work day until the time you leave for home, you should strive to be reasonably productive.

In the business of billing hours for services to clients, a reasonably productive employee works diligently and correctly charges their time to the applicable client's job. If the employee is at the office for nine hours during the day and takes an hour for lunch, eight hours should be charged and allocated to the jobs being worked on, provided the employee is reasonably productive.

Reasonable productivity is where the employee is making an honest, diligent attempt to process the job in the most efficient and effective manner possible. Reasonable productivity lies in between an employee who is a superstar at what they do, and the employee who is playing for fun on the Internet. It's an honest day's living.

Don't Reinvent the Wheel

Many people view a new issue as if they are the first person to deal with the issue. The simple fact is that most things that are new to us are not new at all; many other people have already dealt with this same thing in the past. Consultants are naturally focused on taking on new challenges and usually have a strong desire to solve the problem their own way. This is not a bad characteristic to possess, but significant time can be saved if you first find out if others have dealt with this issue before.

An email or call to others within your company is a great way to ask if anyone else has dealt with a similar issue. If you find someone who has dealt with a similar issue, you could save significant time by leveraging on their past experience. Ask for a copy of their work product and correspondence to understand how they handled the issue and the

PART 4: WORKING SMART

related facts and conclusions that were reached. It's also important to have personal conversations with others who have dealt with the issue. If this is properly done, you will probably achieve about 70 percent of the information you need to solve the problem or resolve the issue you're working on. You will also have the opportunity of making the client work product even better than it was before, because this leveraging of knowledge will give you additional time to think about new ideas and additional information that can be incorporated into your work product.

The key is to spend a sufficient amount of time upfront researching if someone else has already turned the wheel on the problem or issue you are confronting. As we all know, other employees in the company are all busy solving their own problems and issues, so you need to be very specific about what you're requesting, and you, not them, will need to exert the energy to find the comparative work product. For example, if you ask the other employee to give you a copy of relevant comparative work, they may provide it if it's as simple as clicking the electronic button on the computer. However, if that person has to get out of their chair and start searching in files for your benefit, chances are they simply won't do it. In that case, you'll need to expend the energy necessary to obtain the information. Take the initiative to get out of your chair and find the information when it's not readily available.

It is also prudent to talk to other professionals outside your company to determine if they have ever dealt with the issue or problem that you're dealing with. You can learn a lot by examining how they handled the issue and what conclusions were reached. You will also have the benefit of seeing how the conclusions played out in real life, so you can make better decisions in regard to your own issue.

A prudent company will expand the resources necessary to compile and organize the current and historical work that all the employees have produced over the years. This database should be organized in electronic files so that all employees can easily research and gain access to the information. Many companies simply store the old jobs that the employees have done in the past in offsite boxes, and very few employees in the company will actually go that far to search for old jobs that could be helpful to their current situation. I have a saying for the younger generation that grew up using computers: "If it's not on the computer screen, it simply does not exist." In other words, they're not willing to go search through boxes full of paper to determine if what they are currently working on has been done in the past. In order to close this information gap, a prudent company will develop an electronic database of all prior jobs to minimize the reinventing-the-wheel syndrome.

My company is currently developing an electronic intranet "knowledge base" that will have all relevant work documents organized in a meaningful fashion so that employees can fully leverage the past experience of others in the company. This gives each employee tremendous knowledge available at their fingertips, creates company franchise value, and provides the clients we are serving with a more effective product at a better price.

Drill the Job to Its Fullest

Drilling a job to its fullest refers to the notion that the employee who performs services for a client contributes every meaningful thought and idea to the job at hand with the goal of providing as much value-added service as possible to the client and the client's project. Drilling a job is not milking a job for consulting dollars—if a company operated this way, its prospects for future growth and subsistence would be doubtful. Employees don't view the job as something that has a start and finish date, but as a continuum

PART 4: WORKING SMART

because striving to provide meaningful thoughts and ideas to the client is never-ending.

Clients operate with budgets for each job, but the administrative aspects of a budget become secondary when the client realizes they have engaged a consultant who continues to add value to the job every step of the way. Drilling a job means treating the job as if it's the only one you have, carefully thinking about and discussing with the client all ideas and opportunities. If you're in a hurry to get the job done so you can move on to the next job, you are not drilling the job, you are simply processing the job.

An employee who properly drills a job on behalf of a client becomes permanently connected to the job because they become so familiar and knowledgeable about it. In the real estate consulting business, the permanent fixture analogy is akin to "running with the land or the real estate project" because the client's employees will turn over occasionally, but the consultant that properly drills the job will always be an instrumental part of the project.

There are a multitude of attributes associated with a consultant who successfully drills the job for their client's benefit. One attribute is always discussing in detail with the client the issues and obstacles associated with the job. You must squeeze as much information out of the client as you can in order to develop a solid understanding of the issues and obstacles, at least from the client's perspective. This background-gathering puts you in the right position to start developing good ideas or solutions for your client.

The second attribute of a successful job driller is that the employee will always power through the obstacles in front of them in order to achieve the job goals. The more successful you are at moving job obstacles out of the way, the deeper you will drill into other opportunities of the job that can allow you to add more value.

The third attribute is a perspective that you are not only performing the specific work the client expects, but are also looking for other value-added opportunities. For example, assume one of the source documents you need to review for the client's benefit is a land development budget. As you review the budget, you may see other opportunities that could add even more value for the client, in addition to the value you plan to add for the specific job at hand. You may see that the land development budget is missing certain costs or some of the cost estimates are inaccurate. There may be costs in the budget that should have a reimbursement or credit opportunity because of the unique circumstances. This type of horizontal drilling demonstrates to the client that you are viewing the job as if you are an owner and not just another consultant.

Additional attributes consist of being organized on the job, never quitting until the issue is resolved satisfactorily, having a good to do list that serves to root out all the opportunities, and continually communicating with the client in a manner that shows a genuine interest in getting the optimal benefit for the client.

Don't Give Information—Get it

Better information or intelligence about a topic puts you in the position to achieve more than another person who does not have the information. When negotiating against someone who has a lower level of knowledge or fewer facts, you will usually come out on top because the other person may not fully understand what they are giving up and what they are receiving. The power of negotiating is

PART 4: WORKING SMART

directly related to the degree of information, knowledge, and facts that you have regarding the subject you're negotiating.

It takes a long time to build a solid database of information and facts for the industry you work in. I always think of military tactics when I think of this topic, in that the military with the best intelligence about its opposition is usually best positioned to know when to strike its opponent and fully capitalize on the intelligence they have. In the first Gulf War with Iraq, the U.S. knew that the stealth fighter plane technology was an advantage they had over their opposition. The opposition didn't have a way to identify these fighters, so it was logical to stage the initial attacks by using the stealth fighter planes to knock out Iraq's air defense system and pave the way for other more identifiable planes.

Building intelligence in the services business doesn't just consist of creating a database of as many facts about a subject as possible. It also requires that you database the personal profiles of the people you are working for and against in a business transaction, primarily from the perspective of the positions they usually take on various issues related to the business transaction. For example, you may have worked with an attorney on a prior transaction related to the current transaction you're involved in. The information you previously gained from the attorney relative to his or her position on certain issues should be extremely useful as you plan your dealings with this attorney in the current transaction.

You should consciously build your intelligence database on a daily basis. This involves asking lots of questions to understand as much as possible about the topic that you are dealing with. When someone, especially on the other side of the negotiation, pumps you for information, you should attempt to answer their question in a way that protects the information or intelligence you have. Answer the question as accurately and honestly as possible to maintain your professional credibility, but avoid giving away elements of your information database. If you are ineffective at doing this, you will appear untrustworthy, and any leverage you may have had in the negotiation will be lost. Trust in negotiating with someone is paramount, and you cannot afford to lose it.

The reason for guarding your intelligence is that it takes a long time to obtain it, so why would you want to hand it to others who may potentially use it against you? Let them take their own time and energy to get the relevant information or intelligence they may need in conducting a negotiation. While they are trying to get information you already have, you will be figuring out how to plan the negotiation approach, so, by definition, you are staying one step ahead of your opposition in the negotiation.

Now there are times in a negotiation that you want to give certain information to the opposing side in an effort to draw them down a path that would logically lead them to the conclusions you want them to come to. In doing this, a lot of time can be saved and the negotiation may get done more quickly than otherwise, which could be an important benefit to your client.

Over time, people that you negotiate with will start to figure out that you excel at gathering facts and intelligence about the topic you are negotiating on, and because of this you will actually build stronger professional credibility. However, the opposing side will also attempt to get more and more information from you, and you must simply hold the line.

PART 4: WORKING SMART

– 62 –
Don't Build a Mountain Out of a Molehill

People sometimes have a tendency to overdo things and do much more work than they really need to. Some people are just simply not smart enough or experienced enough to boil through what they're trying to accomplish, so it just takes them longer to get things done. Everyone works at different speeds, and it's perfectly acceptable that it takes someone longer to do something, so long as they're not adding unnecessary tasks or causing someone else to pay for their inefficiency. Others go out of their way to make simple things complicated because it gives them a feeling of power and control. Personally, I think people who make things more complex than need be simply have too much time on their hands.

In the services business, a consultant should do only what is necessary to get the job done—nothing more or nothing less. The client should not be expected to pay for unnecessary consultant time. For example, if the consultant is doing a task that doesn't reasonably relate to the job, the client should not be expected to pay for the time incurred. Sometimes consultants do much more work on a job than they need to because they have little else to work on or perhaps they just overanalyze what's necessary to get the job done.

Overanalyzing is a common problem in the consulting business, and it's up to the management in the consulting company to properly train the consultants to do only what is necessary. I call it building a mountain out of a molehill with no real purpose in mind. New and inexperienced consultants often don't have enough time on the job to fully understand how much time and energy should be put into the job, so it is management's responsibility to properly monitor and teach these consultants and ensure that they are only doing what's necessary to complete the job.

CONSULTANT, CONSULT!

If the teaching is done properly, after a few years the new consultant will be well-groomed and very efficient and effective.

Things get much more difficult for a consulting company when they have employees in management who still overanalyze jobs. Bad habits allowed to continue over a long period of time are much harder to break than those stopped early on. Chances are that if a consultant has been overanalyzing jobs for years, it will be difficult for them to break this bad habit, but it can be done with good coaching from peers.

The consulting company has an obligation to its clients to make sure it is doing everything possible to break consultants' bad habits of analysis paralysis or building mountains out of molehills at the client's expense. These problems are like cancer to a company and must be removed quickly before they spread to other employees. You can be assured that a consultant who has this problem will always exceed every budget set for the jobs they work on, adding pressure to the company-client relationship.

Some of the ways a company can identify consultants who have this problem are by talking to others within the company and by reviewing employee evaluations, which are usually done annually. After identifying a consultant with this problem, the company should clearly set specific expectations to resolve the problem and a timeframe to see real improvement. Some will change and others will not because they operate in a linear fashion; the latter should probably be counseled out of the consulting business because they are just not cut out for this work.

PART 4: WORKING SMART

– 63 – Write Your Business Biography Now

I recently watched a biography of Benjamin Franklin on the History Channel. Franklin had so many accomplishments, from being a great diplomat instrumental in establishing treaties during the Revolutionary War, to creating the U.S. Constitution, to being a wonderful scientist who invented many things well ahead of his time.

I don't know about you, but I get fired up and inspired when I watch biographies of people like Benjamin Franklin. I get renewed energy to dream a little and set new goals for myself. As I listened in awe to all the great accomplishments that Franklin achieved in his lifetime, I began to reflect upon myself and the accomplishments I have achieved to date. I also realized that most people don't have role models. Have you noticed that when someone achieves success, they always refer to someone who was an inspiration or role model for them? For instance, great modern day musicians often refer to the Beatles or others as their early sources of inspiration. This connection with a role model gives them the added drive and energy to propel them toward achieving their goals.

I believe every consultant should identify one or more role models who provide them with the added inspiration to perform their job well. Over time, this inspiration will turn into purpose-driven passion, which is a powerful personal character trait.

At first glance, you might wonder what you and Benjamin Franklin have in common as it relates to the business world. One could be that you want to be known as a great negotiator. Maybe you want to be known as an inventor of new ideas or work products that are cutting-edge and new to your industry. Or perhaps you want to be known as a great problem-solver or thinker.

Of course, Benjamin Franklin is a hard act to follow, but in your own way you can set lofty goals for yourself. Set goals in terms of what you want to achieve and be known for in business. No one else can do this for you. *You* have to set the goals and find the inspiration.

In writing out or living out your business biography, visualize your elderly self sitting in a rocking chair, reflecting on the things you accomplished in business. What do you hope to have accomplished by the time you retire? It's like writing a script for a movie about your life in business. Then go and live out that script and accomplish your loftiest goals over time.

Another approach is to simply visualize what you want to be recognized for when you retire from your business. What will your company have to say about your accomplishments at your retirement party? Even if you end up not accomplishing all the things you had in mind during your career, at least you tried, which is far better than not trying.

Don't wait to script your business biography. Do it now, because the show will go on with or without you. Don't sit on the sidelines and be a spectator watching the show. Script a leading role for yourself!

Here's an outline you may want to use to get started:

We're here today to honor <your name>, who is retiring after a distinguished career as an industry consultant.

Over the years, <your name> looked to _____, _____, and _____ as role models.

PART 4: WORKING SMART

Not surprisingly, like those role models, <your name> enjoyed a great deal of success.

*<Your name> was especially successful _____
_____
_____
_____.*

*As well, <your name> _____
_____
_____
_____.*

Anyone who has known and worked with <your name> has been impressed with his/her sterling character, especially his/her _____, _____, and _____.

True to form, <your name> has served as a positive role model for many gathered here today. Now it's my honor and privilege to invite three colleagues of <your name> to come to the podium to express their words of appreciation to <your name>.

64. Teach with Analogies and Parables

Do you recall in your high school or college days asking yourself what in the world your textbooks were talking about? Maybe you thought, *How on earth will this material ever apply to my life?* I recently helped my daughter with her math equations. I tried to explain the purpose of each math equation in terms of how it relates to real-world situations. I also told her that in order to really understand and remember the equations, she needed to relate them in ways that made sense to her. Unfortunately, at the ripe age of 12 she was more interested in just getting done with her homework so she could do something more interesting.

There isn't a day that goes by where we don't learn something new and different. Learning can really be solidified when taught with analogies and parables. The information is more firmly rooted in your mind when it is learned with analogies and parables. If a good analogy or parable is utilized, the student will remember it forever.

In business, employees are always working so fast to process all the information they need in order to do their job well. A prudent manager will slow down and take the time to properly teach and train the employees beneath them. One of the manager's goals should be to clearly and concisely communicate information to his or her employees so that they understand it the first time. Nothing is more frustrating than having to teach the same thing over and over to the same employee, because, for whatever reason, the employee is just not digesting, retaining, or applying the information properly and consistently.

In my experience, teaching with analogies or parables is an excellent way of transferring knowledge and information to others and has the greatest chance of sticking in the employee's mind in the first session. Since you probably have a sense of the employee's knowledge base, it makes sense to relate any new information back to the information they already know through an analogy. This gives the employee a much better chance of retaining and understanding the new information the first time.

I actually prefer using parables over analogies because you teach the information as a story, and people can relate to stories. But teaching with parables goes a step further, in that each parable has a moral to the story that attempts to distinguish right from wrong. In business,

PART 4: WORKING SMART

the moral to the story helps the employee understand the proper ways in which the information should and shouldn't be used on projects. Teaching with parables takes a lot of practice, but like anything else, the more you do it the better you get at it. It also consumes much of the manager's time initially, but over the long term it will pay off in spades because the "student" employee will be able to clearly link the stories together to form a comprehensive picture of what they're doing in their job and how it relates to their client's business.

If the employee being taught is not able to fully grasp the analogies or parables you used in teaching them, you may not want to waste your time teaching them this way. You may need to question their aptitude in order to determine if the consulting business is really right for them. Every teacher wants to make their teaching count, and nothing is worse than trying to teach someone who's not interested or just isn't getting it. Remember that your parables must be good or the employee might become bored and stop listening.

CONSULTANT, CONSULT!

PART 5
PURSUE EXCELLENCE

CONSULTANT, CONSULT!

PART 5: PURSUE EXCELLENCE

65 – How Did You Make a Difference Today?

Look around the workforce and you will see people going through the daily motions of their jobs without exerting any true meaning, conviction, or passion behind their work efforts. At the end of each workday, these same people readily admit to friends and spouses that they accomplished little during their day on the job. Some people openly admit they don't even like their job. Obviously, if you don't like your job or have little regard for your job, you will not perform well in your job.

Rather than use excuses about why they do not like their job, it would be wise for employees to instead look into the mirror and realize that their attitude and effort are the primary reason for not performing well on the job. It's easy to blame everything else and everybody else when things aren't going the way you think they should. It's also easy to let unhappiness in your personal life carry over into your work life, affecting your performance. A careless attitude will eventually result in a bad attitude toward your job, and at that point, it's difficult to turn things around.

There is an obvious correlation between the passion applied in your daily work and the results you achieve from such work. The simple adage, "What you put into it is what you get out of it," most certainly applies here. Don't think your lack of passion in your work goes unnoticed. Most employers are constantly looking for passionate employees within their workforce so they can build these employees into future leaders in the company.

CONSULTANT, CONSULT!

To succeed in your job, you need to continually grow and to make a tangible difference on a daily basis. You should ask yourself, "What did I do today that made a positive contribution to my company or my client?"

At my firm, we train our consultants to perform tasks or services for clients that result in obtaining income, reducing costs, or controlling or reducing business risk. Every service must contain one or more of the three desired results. This simple credo helps keep our consultants focused on striving to do things that bring tangible daily results for our clients. To be an effective consultant, you must continually challenge yourself to make a difference in your day-to-day work.

Making a positive difference can be manifested in many different ways. An internal IT person can develop better ways for his or her company to process business more effectively, efficiently, and securely. A consultant can develop new ideas or create new market opportunities that can increase the profit of his or her client's bottom line.

To survive and thrive on a job—whatever the job may be in terms of complexity or responsibility—you must force yourself to create the opportunities that positively enhance the company's future. This will undoubtedly provide you a great future with your company and an opportunity to increase your personal wealth.

Of course, as noted in an earlier chapter, some employers fail to recognize and acknowledge high achievers, and if this applies to you, it may be time to consider moving on to an employer who will better recognize you for your contributions. But you must be realistic and honest with yourself about your true capabilities when making a decision to move on from your current employer.

PART 5: PURSUE EXCELLENCE

66. Your Name and Your Reputation Are All You Have

In the professional consulting business, it takes many years of hard work to establish an impressive reputation. You earn your name and reputation by conducting hundreds of meetings and contributing a vast array of high-quality content over a long period of time to the business circuits in which you circulate. Being consistently accurate in how you communicate your information is also beneficial.

Unfortunately, it doesn't take long to damage your name and reputation if you perform substandard work. Of course, if a consultant rarely performs work of excellence they will never be afforded the opportunity of earning a name or reputation for themselves. Consultants of this type will usually move from one job to another not realizing that the reason they haven't been consistently successful is not the job—it's them.

A successful consultant must always uphold and defend their name and reputation. Speak for yourself and never let others put words in your mouth. I remember a meeting where one of the participants started making certain statements on my behalf that were inaccurate. I respectfully clarified what this person was attempting to say and explained in my own words the statements that I believed to be accurate, even though it was not as beneficial to my client. If I had simply sat there and said nothing to clarify the statements, I ran the risk of losing credibility and of tarnishing my reputation and name. Ironically, your client will appreciate your professional integrity in conducting business and will probably give you more business to work on in the future.

CONSULTANT, CONSULT!

Oftentimes, meeting participants assume that if you don't disagree or provide clarification to an issue or topic then you must support or agree with it. Silence does not earn you a name or reputation, so if you don't agree with something, you should state it for the record and provide alternative solutions for consideration.

I realize there are times when parties are in the process of agreeing with something that is beneficial to your client and you must in most cases simply bite your tongue. The only exception to this would be if they were agreeing to something egregiously wrong. Then you should openly provide your opinion as to why that is not an appropriate thing to do. If your concerns fall on deaf ears, you may want to consider putting them in writing and possibly disassociating yourself from the job.

There may be others times that another consulting firm is challenging and degrading your work. In this case, you must rise to the challenge and vehemently defend your work. This should be no problem to do if you performed the work with quality and professionalism as you should always do.

Also, don't just blindly sign off on things that are brought for your review and/or approval. Your signature or sign-off on work is your personal endorsement, which is directly related to your professional reputation when it comes to business matters.

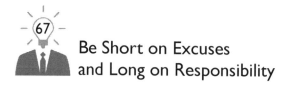

Be Short on Excuses and Long on Responsibility

The world is full of people who simply have an excuse for everything. They become experts at articulating all the reasons and rationale as

PART 5: PURSUE EXCELLENCE

to why they are unable to achieve. Making excuses becomes a compulsive behavioral trait if not nipped in the bud. If you surround yourself with other people with similar traits, it magnifies and gets even worse. In business, people do not take kindly to others who always have an excuse for why something is not getting done. It's simply not an acceptable means of conducting business. Now I realize there are times when there are honest reasons behind why something is not getting done, but this must be communicated in a way that allows the other person to believe it's not just another excuse. The person in business who's full of excuses and never achieves any meaningful results will ultimately be fired. The company cannot afford to let this type of person bring others down. It's like a cancer that damages the company culture.

Consultants must eliminate the excuse card from their daily conduct and instead focus on increasing their responsibility on the job at hand. You should always attempt to exceed the client's job expectations. Always getting the job done on time or in advance is an excellent way of demonstrating job responsibility. Deploying complete persistence and conviction toward solving your client's problems is another way.

Clients can sense how dedicated a consultant is to the client's cause by the actions or inactions of the consultant. Showing that you are not going to quit until the problem is resolved is always appreciated by the client. Working late into the evening to deliver client results for the client's early morning meeting exhibits responsibility. When a client continues to come back with more work, this is an excellent indication that they view you as a responsible consultant. This is another way of them telling you that you are their go-to person.

Responsibility means always being there for the client when they need you. It's not a fair-weathered client relationship in that the timing of the client's needs should not be driven by the consultant's availability or lack thereof. A prudent consultant will always be there when the client needs them, and if for some reason you cannot be there, then you should take the responsibility to make sure another person from your company can handle the client's needs on the client's timeline.

I realize scheduling conflicts may arise and you must force yourself to take on the most important client-related matters. For example, if a client needs you to attend an important meeting on a job you have been working on, it's more important to go to the meeting than to go to some lesser engagement that is conflicting with your schedule such as attending a client lunch, seminar, or initial kick-off meeting. Someone else in the company can go to these functions in your place.

On some occasions, however, I find that consultants use scheduling conflicts as an excuse for why they cannot be there when the client needs them. I often question if they are truly being responsible to their client or if they are simply fearful of what the responsibility entails. Responsibility does not come without pressure, so the sooner you realize this and get over it the better you will become as a consultant. Just think of all the character you are building in yourself by being responsible.

Continually Develop New Ideas— Don't Just Rely on Old Ones

We see things changing all the time in our environment—all based on the implementation of new technologies that stem from someone's good idea. We are fortunate in America that we have lots of creative people who are always thinking of better ways to do

PART 5: PURSUE EXCELLENCE

something. Sometimes change is met with resistance because it can negatively change the economic picture of the incumbent. The fact is that if you don't continue to evolve and develop new ways of doing things better, the world will pass you by.

Whether we like it or not, America has been evolving from a manufacturing economy to a service economy, and this only increases the pressure to be a leader in developing good ideas that create sound economies and efficiencies. Business cycles change from good times to bad times. The services a consulting firm offers may be in high demand in good economic times but have little demand in bad economic times. A prudent consulting firm will always provide services that are needed in both good and bad economic times, and these services will often be different. Mortgage companies are an example of a business model that goes boom-to-bust when real estate markets go up and down. The fundamental problem is that most of these mortgage companies are unable to build or retain customer loyalty from year-to-year because they have mostly one-time customers.

Clients appreciate a consultant who is always coming up with refinements to existing ideas or developing new ideas that can add value to their bottom line. Anytime an industry is in transition you should ask yourself, "What are the smart things I should be telling my clients?"

In order to develop new ideas, you should have a learning process in place to increase your technical competency on a daily or weekly basis. The consultant should make a regular habit of reviewing best-in-class books and documents that are germane to the services they perform.

The consultant may also want to consider reviewing books or information about industries that have strong corollaries to the industry they are working in, especially if one industry is more advanced or refined than others. For example, there might be something to learn or use from the manufacturing process of making an automobile that could make the process of constructing a house more cost-effectively.

You also may want to look at a client's agreement on a certain transaction and develop ideas about what they could do or not do to enhance their economic position. Most people in business simply file their agreement away, failing to realize that certain events may transpire in the future that could have an impact on such an agreement. A lot of agreements discuss the possibility of events that may arise in the future and how the economics of the agreement could change if certain events actually occurred.

Always Lead

In my mind, a leader is someone who strives for excellence in everything they do. A leader leads by example. Talk is cheap; actions are everything.

I remember discussing a special work product that our company was developing for our clients with an associate who was involved in developing the product. The associate believed the product would be beneficial for our clients. However, due to personality conflicts, the associate was not fully engaging with the company involved in the project. I explained to the associate that a leader needs to set aside personality conflicts and any other distractions in the spirit of doing the right thing—meeting client needs.

A leader does not let anything get in the way of doing the right thing. In fact, one of the very first questions that should be addressed in the mind of a leader is, "What is the right thing to do?"

PART 5: PURSUE EXCELLENCE

Sometimes I have to laugh when the media portrays some individuals as societal leaders when in reality they are followers. I personally don't think a Hollywood movie star, a newscaster, or a politician is a leader within society, although the media sure portrays them this way.

A leader's primary goal should be to instill leadership skills in others so that they in turn become leaders. At my company, we hold internal seminars periodically for the purpose of accelerating the transfer of knowledge to employees. Our goal is to have senior management provide meaningful information so that employees are able to increase competency through real-world experiences. It seems to be working well at our company because I get other competing consultants complimenting upper management for how quickly new hires are downloaded with information that helps them perform well in their jobs.

A competing consultant once told me that he couldn't believe how much one of our entry-level consultants knew though he only had one year of work experience with our firm. The competing consultant claimed that he had been working with the competing company for three years and was just now beginning to go to client meetings. He told me this because he was interviewing with our firm for a job. This was a nice compliment that indicated we were doing a good job in leading our personnel in this particular area.

Whatever you do, learn to be a leader. Then instill your leadership skills in others. It will sharpen your skills and accelerate your rise to the top.

CONSULTANT, CONSULT!

- 70 -
Never Say or Do These Things in Business

In business, protect your professionalism. Whether you like it or not, your employer is evaluating and judging your abilities daily. Avoid showing tentativeness toward taking on new and different challenges. How can you grow professionally if you don't take on more job responsibilities over time? If you're interested in accelerating your professional career path, then be willing to take on work outside your ordinary comfort zones.

Never hand in work without a thorough review of the content for logic, spelling, and grammatical errors. Remember that once you hand over your work, it is considered to be a product of your competence. Re-read your product twice if need be to make sure that you have taken the necessary steps to show the competence of your work to your supervisor. Your work product has your personal signature on it and you should always hold it in the highest regard.

Take an honest account of your work schedule and avoid taking on additional work that you know you will be unable to complete in a timely manner. Know your limits and remember not to stretch yourself too thin so that it begins to compromise the quality of the work you produce. While your intentions might be good, you certainly don't want a supervisor to think of you as a hindrance rather than an asset, so make sure you are truly able to dedicate the proper amount of time to a task before asking for or accepting additional responsibilities.

Never leave a meeting without a clear understanding of the full scope of responsibilities and duties that are associated with the task that has been given to you. Concentrate on the entire dialogue in the meeting; you never know what you will be expected to retain

PART 5: PURSUE EXCELLENCE

about the conversation so pay attention and ask questions if you are unfamiliar with a subject in the conversation. You will quickly lose favor with your supervisor if he or she does not feel you have retained the information presented to you.

Never assume that a responsibility that was given to a member of your team was taken care of. Following up with that team member is a must. It is imperative that if your supervisor comes to you for an update on the task that you can give a detailed and competent answer to any questions that they pose. Remember that as a team leader, the responsibility for the completion of that task will ultimately fall on your shoulders.

There is a difference between talking badly about colleagues and constructive criticism. Never talk badly about your colleagues. It's a simple rule that at times can get overlooked, but remember to always think about the implications that your words will have. Not everyone will agree with your perception of that colleague and you run the risk of your fellow colleagues thinking that you are unprofessional and disrespectful. If you talk badly about one colleague, it typically means that you have spoken negatively about others as well. Don't be the curator of the gossip mill in your firm. It is a temptation that is at times difficult to avoid but in order to maintain the trust of your colleagues you must avoid it at all costs. The negativity that it breeds will ultimately have far-reaching implications on the overall health of your firm.

Never be late for a meeting. Being late will instill a sense of anxiety in your client as to whether or not you have the competence and proper time-management skills to complete the task at hand. This sends a powerful message to your client that you truly do not value their time. How can you be trusted with the tasks that will be asked of you if you are not able to complete the simplest of tasks—showing up on time? Remember that showing up 10 minutes early to a meeting is actually considered to be on-time, while showing up at the exact time of your meeting is considered to be late. While you have met your deadline, you have failed to provide ample time for all parties to exchange information, pass out all relevant documentation, and set up the agenda for the meeting. Simply put: Don't be late. Period! Time is money, so set an example for your team and be punctual.

Lastly, a consultant should never attempt to part with projects. Don't burden others with work you're unwilling to do. This behavior demonstrates a lack of commitment and responsibility to your job, your employer, and your client. Working on a job and finishing it shows persistence and determination.

71 - Always Exceed Client Expectations

Normally, people do only what is necessary to get by. Sometimes that is acceptable, but most times it's not. Many people will gauge their level of participation based on what others have done in the past. If the bar has been set to a low standard, then most people will simply work with this standard and consider it acceptable. Likewise, if the bar has been set to a high standard, then most people will establish this standard as the expectation threshold. While sometimes it is appropriate to match the historical standards that have been applied to certain circumstances, at other times it is inappropriate.

There may be situations where a higher standard is in order, and each person has an opportunity to set this higher standard. The first thing the person needs to do is recognize that the opportunity exists. Opportunities are like doors in that they open and close, and if you're not insightful enough to act on opportunities

PART 5: PURSUE EXCELLENCE

in a timely manner, then it may be too late. In everything you do, you should always ask yourself, *What is the expectation level that the business world has set on what I'm working on?* And then you should ask yourself, *What can I do to make it better?* You should take the time to stop and think about the job you are working on in order to figure out the specific things you can do to make it exceed the expectation level of your client. Implementing ideas that add more value to the client's bottom line than the client expected is always good. Getting your job done sooner than the client expected is also good.

A good manager will train employees to strive for excellence. There will be times, however, when a client has unrealistic expectations. It is then your obligation to consult with the client to understand their intent and goals, and then come up with realistic expectations. If the client is unwilling to accept modified expectations, then the consultant should seriously consider telling the client that they cannot perform the requested job.

Of course, a client's expectations may be mixed. Be sure to identify all of the stakeholders. Determine if they agree on what's expected. If the stakeholders disagree on expectations, don't panic. Part of your job as a consultant is to help clients clarify their objectives, goals, and standards. Often, doing this is just as important as completing the job itself. If two or more stakeholders continue to strongly disagree or differ on expectations, you may need to tap your supervisor's wisdom and experience. Again, don't panic. This could be an opportunity to exceed your client's expectations.

In your own work, look for opportunities to innovate. If there is a better way to do something and you determine it is cost-beneficial, try it. Take the time to stop and think about the job you are working on and figure out the specific things you can do to exceed client expectations. If the client doesn't acknowledge your exceptional work, then dialogue to determine if they had a different set of expectations in mind. If a client is short on giving you feedback, but they continue to give you more jobs to work on, however, this action is an unspoken endorsement that you're meeting or exceeding their expectations. Keep up the good work.

Never forget that excellence isn't accidental. Always do more than expected. In the end, you'll be the winner.

72 — Don't Take on Work You Cannot Finish on Time

It's great to take on more work and responsibilities. This demonstrates a solid commitment to the company and clients. If you seek to exceed expectations regularly, you'll typically always have lots of work to do. However, as projects begin to pile up it might start becoming a challenge to get everything done, even if you're working long hours. At times like this, it can be tempting to cut corners for the sake of finishing a project. This hurts both the company and you. Additionally, others in the company may lose the opportunity to learn if you're hording work.

If the work is not getting done on time, you begin to lose credibility. Others who have relied on you begin to become affected and develop negative attitudes. A smart consultant knows when to draw the line. Always ask lots of questions before taking on additional projects. Some questions to consider asking are:

- Where am I at with my current jobs in terms of remaining work hours to finish?
- Is the new job complex or relatively simple?

PART 5: PURSUE EXCELLENCE

- Who am I working for (both internal management and client), and are they reasonable or difficult to work with?
- Is the expectation of timeframe for completion consistent with my expectations?
- Who else can I use to assist in the job's completion?
- Do the assistant consultants have strong or weak job experience relative to the work being taken on?

Consider who else on the team might benefit from helping with the project. If you believe it's simply not possible to meet the expectations of those who are asking you to take on the new job, then you must say "no."

Sometimes saying "no" to additional projects can be perceived as unwillingness or a lack of commitment. However, since it is important to finish projects on time, your ability to complete the project in a timely manner should always be a consideration when thinking about taking on more work. Over time, strive to learn how to recruit others to help with projects, ensuring lots of work now and in the future.

An experienced consultant sets clear expectations for those working on the job, places significant responsibility on them to make sure things go smoothly, and gets the job done on time. As well, seasoned consultants learn to manage co-workers by demonstrating leadership and dedication—two of the quickest ways to move vertically within the company.

So, should you take on more work at this point? Yes, if you're able and you're ready to take another step up in your career. But never take on work you cannot finish on time.

CONSULTANT, CONSULT!

73. The Incremental Difference Will Set You Apart from Others

Working 10 hours a day at your job instead of eight gives you two additional hours of knowledge each day. If an employee does this over the year, the employee will have worked about 2,550 hours over the year compared to a typical employee who would have worked 2,080 hours based on a standard eight-hour day. If the employee does this over 30 years, the employee will have worked about 76,500 hours compared to a typical employee who would have worked 62,400 hours. Over this 30-year timeframe, this represents about 6.8 more years worked by the 10-hour per day employee versus the eight-hour per day employee.

All other things being equal, the employee who works this incremental difference on a daily basis has the opportunity to become on average 23 percent smarter and more experienced than other employees. I learned at an early age—primarily through sporting activities—that if I worked out or practiced harder and longer, then I would have a better chance of beating my competition. If I wanted to run faster, I would focus on workout activities that would help me accomplish my goal, but I also knew I would have to work out incrementally more than my competition in order to gain an advantage.

As the years went by, I simply transferred this "incremental difference" philosophy to my college education, whereby I established my own personal curriculum in addition to the school's curriculum. I had assembled my own personal booklet of thousands of vocabulary words outside the school curriculum in order to improve my speaking and writing skills.

PART 5: PURSUE EXCELLENCE

By the time I entered the business world, my application of the incremental difference philosophy was well embedded in my character. I would get in to work early and read technical information related to the real estate industry. I would listen to audio tapes of technical lectures on the real estate industry as I drove to and from work. On weekends, I would do library research on specific topics I was interested in the real estate field. I would read through as many of these books to understand what has been done in these areas in terms of experience and analysis.

I didn't expect pay for this "incremental difference" because I knew I was investing in my future. I also knew the benefits of my efforts would be realized at some later point in my career. That effort at the beginning of my career definitely has paid off.

The best attributes I obtained has been the development of a solid professional character and reputation and economic gain relative to my peer group. Working harder will provide you with many options, ranging from making more money faster, being smarter than those in your peer group, earning promotions, gaining work responsibilities, and ultimately retiring sooner.

74. You're Only as Good as Your Last Job—Accept It and Move On

Society dictates expectations. If you're a great baseball player, spectators will expect you to perform well in every game. If you play a bad game, there is instant doubt placed on your ability to play well in the future. This is a rather thankless environment to operate in, but the fact is this is what society expects. So accept it.

CONSULTANT, CONSULT!

The pressure and stakes get even higher for the highly-compensated people of the world because society quickly correlates the compensation to the expectation of great performance. A successful person understands and accepts society's grand expectations, but he or she also realizes they are not a robot, and there will be days where their performance will not be up to snuff. A successful person doesn't let success go to his or her head, and they never take anything for granted. They are internally proud of themselves for their accomplishments, but are externally humble.

As an employee, you are expected to do your job well every day. Clients always expect excellence. In my younger years of consulting, I executed a service that ended up saving the client a lot of money. The client expressed sincere appreciation for the resulting work, and I thought a celebration or party was in order. I met with the client the very next day to talk about a new project, and the client had already digested the prior day's success and was ready for the next endeavor. This experience taught me the value of remembering that today's achievements will not necessarily be remembered or rewarded tomorrow. But if you really think about it, a prudent consultant shouldn't be after the glory anyway; instead, they should be making sure they're doing the things that result in getting more work in the future from their client. Certainly, getting good financial results for your client's bottom line is one way of insuring this. A really smart consultant will give the glory of success to the client so that their client looks good within their own company.

A well-managed consulting company will train employees to understand and accept this reality: you're only as good as your last job. The internal system within the consulting company should be structured so that it's not cold and impersonal like the rest of the world, but instead should be supportive and proud of the consultant's accomplishments. The reward system should include both compensation and recognition.

PART 5: PURSUE EXCELLENCE

Recognition for a job well done is deeply satisfying. Recognition can take many forms, including personal praise, public applause, and written documentation added to a consultant's personnel file.

Celebrate the successes of others on your team; recognize those who help you succeed and you'll always get ahead.

But don't forget that success is never final. Every day, make it your objective to win again.

75 — Aptitude Is Everything, But Actually Nothing If You Don't Put It into Action

I can't help but think about college professors when I think about the topic of aptitude. College professors are usually articulate and well-versed in the areas they teach. As you get to know the teacher on a more personal level, however, you sometimes find they have no experience in the area they teach. A person with aptitude who works in a vacuum has little value in the business world.

I am often asked what I look for in potential employees when I interview people. My response is one word: aptitude. However, I add a caveat by saying that the person must put their aptitude into motion so that genuine work-related results are achieved. Aptitude is not necessarily about being textbook smart. Instead it's about being book smart, street smart, a critical thinker, and a problem-solver. Someone of that caliber has a high ceiling of potential. I remember working with a young college graduate from Yale University at the national accounting firm I used to work for. This young man was extremely friendly and often would remind you that he graduated from Yale. His daily work schedule could often be interrupted by doing such things as reading the paper and talking to people in the hallway. As I got to know this young man better, I found that he had good aptitude and was a good critical thinker. I also found that he was rather disengaged and lacked focus; the negative attributes seemed to outweigh the positives so that he ended up being only an average consultant.

In business, there are brilliant employees with tremendous aptitude in the areas they work. Some of these employees put significant energy, drive, and determination behind their aptitude and succeed at almost everything they do. The combined effects of aptitude and the exertion of energy or determination to implement this aptitude makes the employee a formidable force.

On the other hand, there are employees with untapped brilliance. These employees might be lazy, unmotivated, or lack future goals. Nothing is more frustrating for me than to see someone with tremendous aptitude fail to convert their aptitude into meaningful client work product.

Smart companies will value an employee who has less aptitude coupled with tremendous drive and ambition over an employee who has great aptitude with little drive and ambition. Whatever the employee may not have in terms of overall aptitude, they more than make it up with other character traits they possess.

The best employees have it all—aptitude, energy, drive, determination, ambition, and a great track record of success.

It's Your Turn!

The very fact that you read this book suggests you are a consultant or employee with aptitude and ambition. If that is the case, I recommend that you take a few minutes to review the table of contents again. Circle the chapter numbers of any points you intend to review and use to your best advantage. Then write down your top 5 points below. May all 75 principles help you enjoy even more success in the future.

CONSULTANT, CONSULT!

ABOUT THE AUTHOR

John E. Foreman graduated from the business school of Cal State Fullerton with a B.A. degree in Accounting in 1982 and has spent the last 32 years consulting for clients in the real estate industry. Upon graduation, he took his first job with Kenneth Leventhal & Company (KL&CO), a national accounting firm that specialized in the real estate industry and providing audit, tax, and consulting-related services to land developers and builders. While at KL&CO, John worked on a multitude of audit, tax, and consulting projects, serving clients in the real estate industry the first nine years of his career. John obtained his Certified Public Accounting license in 1986 in the State of California.

In 1991, John co-founded the real estate consulting firm Development Planning & Financing Group, Inc., which specializes in providing consulting services to the real estate industry. Under John's leadership and the deployment of the consulting concepts in this book, DPFG has grown to become a highly successful national real estate consulting firm representing some of the most prominent real estate development companies in the nation.

Over the years, John has accumulated significant industry experience in real estate that includes, but is not limited to:

> Valuation of Multiple Land Uses
> Public/Private Sector Negotiations
> Cash Flow Analysis of Projects and Portfolios
> Development Cost Evaluations
> Entitlements to Development

ABOUT THE AUTHOR

> Taxation Strategies
> Public Finance Applications on Development
> Litigation Support
> Redevelopment District Development
> Expert Witness Testimony
> Development Impacts on School Districts
> Land Acquisition Due Diligence
> Project Leasing
> Special Financing District Restructuring
> Auditing of Companies
> Market Analysis and Recommendations
> Operational Analysis of Companies
> Debt/Equity Financing Structures

John has also worked with many notable clients in the real estate arena that include, but are not limited to:

> Bank of America
> Unocal
> The Irvine Company
> Lennar Communities
> BRE Properties
> County of Orange
> Institutional Housing Partners
> Starwood
> Castle & Cooke
> DR Horton
> Capstone Advisors
> Pulte

John's desire is to share his trial and error experiences in consulting to help others improve their job performance and financial success.

CONSULTANT, CONSULT!

ABOUT DEVELOPMENT PLANNING & FINANCING GROUP

Development Planning & Financing Group is committed to providing the real estate development community custom professional services. The firm prides itself on being able to obtain the relevant facts surrounding each transaction and properly advise clients based on such information. The consultants at DPFG are focused on providing services that help land developers, home builders, lenders, investors, and others involved in the real estate industry, navigate the development and construction process in a timely and cost-efficient manner.

DPFG's primary service areas are Arizona, California, Colorado, Idaho, Nevada, North Carolina, South Carolina, Texas, and Florida. DPFG's services are also available to assist the real estate communities in Georgia, Hawaii, New Mexico, Oregon, Utah, Virginia, and Washington.

For more information on DPFG's services and regional offices, please visit www.dpfg.com or call 949-388-9269.

WHAT OTHERS SAY

"John Foreman has challenged me big time with his new book. It's loaded with a wealth of thought-provoking ideas that will elevate your 'game' to a much higher level."
—PAT WILLIAMS, Senior Vice President, Orlando Magic, *and Co-Author of* Takeaway

"John Foreman has captured an essential element that seems to be in short supply in the marketplace today . . . attention to the customer. Foreman provides specific examples of the nuts and bolts of great interaction with clients, attention to detail, and a level of professionalism to which we should all aspire. These 75 principles belong on the desktop of every consultant who's called a pro."
—BILL COPPER, Director of the Hollifield Leadership Center

"Consultant, Consult! is filled with common sense ideas. Each idea can be acted on immediately to improve your personal and business presence."
—LINDA J. MILLER, Global Liaison for Coaching, The Ken Blanchard Companies

CONSULTANT, CONSULT!

"There is a new normal in the 'contract' between employers and employees or consultants, and Foreman has nailed the key elements required for success in today's work environment. As more choose the consultant model, this book will become required reading for those smart and brave enough to walk this path."

—Peter Bourke, *Vice President of Complex Sale, Inc., and Author of A Better Way to Make a Living . . . and a Life, www.betterwaytomakealiving.com*

"I could not put this book down! Both from the client and consulting side of my career, this book makes too much sense. It is an easy read—full of down to earth, successful ideas for being a value-added consultant. You'll learn 75 proven ways to thrive and succeed in today's increasingly competitive world. So, what are you waiting for? Script a leading role for yourself!"

—Jane H. Hubbard, *Retired Director of Organizational Effectiveness,* Delta Air Lines

"Necessary insights for younger consultants, and crucial reminders for experienced ones. Consultant, Consult! *also is a great resource for business people who want to provide greater value at work."*

—Sara Moulton Reger, *IBM Transformation Program Executive, and Author of* Can Two Rights Make a Wrong? *and* Lead and Succeed

WHAT OTHERS SAY

"Consultant, Consult! *is a practical guide for any consultant or organization that hires consultants. The short chapters offer concise advice I could use immediately. John Foreman's stress relief advice to 'resign from being manager of the universe' is a great reminder for Type A entrepreneurs like me. This one was definitely worth the price of admission. Recommended!*"
—J. R. WHITBY, *International Media Consultant*

"*This isn't a book for consultants alone. If only all employees would apply the principles and techniques John Foreman advocates! This is one of the few consulting-related books that is incredibly down-to-earth while adding real value. It was refreshing and easy to read: good reminder of what it takes to give your best.*"
—MARCO BLANKENBURGH, *International Director,* KnowledgeWorkx, *www.knowledgeworkx.com*

"*I love this book!* Consultant, Consult! *delivers a lot more than a prescription for successful consulting. John E. Foreman gives us a treasury of practical business wisdom that will help any consultant or advisor rise to the top, establish long-term client relationships, and build a highly valuable practice.*"
—RON FREY, SR., *Consultant in Management, Marketing, Leadership and Fund-raising*

"*The principles contained in John Foreman's book will help aspiring consultants systematically advance their careers. It also will serve as a manual for all those who aspire to found their own successful firms.*"
—AARON J. CROWLEY, *Business Consultant and Author of* Less Chaos More Cash

Made in the USA
San Bernardino, CA
28 January 2015